THE
BARBADOES GIRL

A Tale for Young People

MRS. HOFLAND

1st WORLD
LIBRARY
Literary Society

The Barbadoes Girl

Mrs. Hofland

© 1st World Library, 2007
PO Box 2211
Fairfield, IA 52556
www.1stworldlibrary.com
First Edition

LCCN: 2007934193

Softcover ISBN: 978-1-4218-9664-9
Hardcover ISBN: 978-1-4218-9764-6
eBook ISBN: 978-1-4218-9564-2

Purchase *"The Barbadoes Girl"*
as a traditional bound book at:
www.1stWorldLibrary.com/purchase.asp?ISBN=978-1-4218-9664-9

1st World Library is a literary, educational organization
dedicated to:

- Creating a free internet library of downloadable ebooks

- Hosting writing competitions and offering book publishing
scholarships.

Interested in more 1st World Library books? contact:
literacy@1stworldlibrary.com
Check us out at: www.1stworldlibrary.com

1ˢᵗ World Library Literary Society

Giving Back to the World

"If you want to work on the core problem, it's early school literacy."

- James Barksdale, former CEO of Netscape

"No skill is more crucial to the future of a child, or to a democratic and prosperous society, than literacy."

- Los Angeles Times

"Literacy... means far more than learning how to read and write... The aim is to transmit... knowledge and promote social participation."

- UNESCO

"Literacy is not a luxury, it is a right and a responsibility. If our world is to meet the challenges of the twenty-first century we must harness the energy and creativity of all our citizens."

- President Bill Clinton

"Parents should be encouraged to read to their children, and teachers should be equipped with all available techniques for teaching literacy, so the varying needs and capacities of individual kids can be taken into account."

- Hugh Mackay

The indulgence of passion makes bitter work for repentance, and produces a feeble old age.

—BACON

As violent contrary winds endanger a ship, so it is with turbulent emotions in the mind; whereas such as are favourable awaken the understanding, keep in motion the will, and make the whole man more vigorous.

—ADDISON

CHAPTER I

As Mr. Harewood was one evening sitting with his wife and children, he told them that he expected soon to receive among them the daughter of a friend, who had lately died in the West Indies.

Mr. Harewood's family consisted of his wife, two sons, and a daughter: the eldest, named Edmund, was about twelve years of age; Charles, the second, was scarcely ten; and Ellen, the daughter, had just passed her eighth birthday: they were all sensible, affectionate children, but a little different in disposition, the eldest being grave and studious, the second lively and active, and as he was nearer to Ellen's age, she was often inclined to romp with him, when she should have minded her book; but she was so fond of her mamma, and was educated with such a proper sense of the duty and obedience she owed her, that a word or a look never failed to restrain the exuberance of her spirits.

Children are alike naturally curious and fond of society; the moment, therefore, Mr. Harewood mentioned their expected guest, every one had some question to ask respecting her; but as Ellen's was uttered with most mildness and modesty, she was first answered; and her brother Charles, taking this hint, listened quietly to the following conversation, not joining in it, till he felt that he had a right to do so, from having practised a forbearance that cost him some effort.

Ellen.—Pray, papa, what is this little girl's name, and how old is she?

Father.—She is called Matilda Sophia Hanson: her father was a man of good fortune, and she is an only child; I believe, however, his affairs are in an unsettled state, as her mother is under the necessity of remaining some time in the country, in order to settle them. It is at her earnest request that I have been prevailed upon to accept the charge of her daughter. I believe she is about a year younger than you; but as the growth of people in warm countries is more rapid than in this, I expect to see her quite as tall and forward as you, Ellen.

Ellen.—But, dear papa, how will she get here from a place on the other side of the globe? I mean, who will bring her? for I know, of course, that she must come in a ship.

Father.—She will be attended by a negro servant, who has always waited upon her; and who will return after she is safely landed, I suppose.

Ellen.—Poor thing! how she will cry when she leaves her own dear mamma, when she is to cross the wide sea! and then again, when she parts with her good nurse; I dare say she will kiss her very fondly, though she is a black.

Charles.—Oh, she will forget her sorrow when she sees so many things that are quite new to her. I'm afraid she'll think Ellen, and us boys, very silly, ignorant creatures, compared to her, who has seen so much of the world: upon my word, we must be all upon our good behaviour.

Father.—I hope you will behave well, not merely from

Mrs. Hofland

conscious inferiority, but because you would be both impolite and unkind, if you omitted any thing in your power that could render a stranger happy, who is so entirely thrown upon our protection—one, too, who has lost a fond father, and is parted from a tender mother.

Edmund.—But, papa, as Miss Hanson is coming to England for education, and is yet very young, surely Charles must be wrong in supposing that she is wiser, or, I ought to say, better informed, than we are, since it is utterly improbable that she should have had the benefit of such instructions as we have enjoyed.

Father.—True, my dear; but yet she will, of course, be acquainted with many things to which you are necessarily entire strangers, although I must remark that Charles's expression, "she has seen much of the world," is not proper; for it is only applied to people who have mixed much with society—not to those whose travels have shown them only land and water. However, coming from a distant country, a society very different from ours, and people to whom you are strangers, she cannot fail to possess many ideas and much knowledge which are unknown to you; I therefore hope her residence with us for a time will prove mutually advantageous; but if the advantage should prove to be on your side, I trust you will never abuse it by laughing, or in any way insulting and teazing your visitant; such conduct would ensure most serious displeasure.

Mother.—It would prove them not only very ignorant, and deficient in the education which even savages give their children, but prove that they were devoid of that spirit of courtesy which is recommended in the Scriptures, and which every Christian child will nourish in his heart and display in his manners: the same holy apostle, who inculcated the highest doctrines of his Divine Master, says also— "Be affable, be courteous, bearing one with another."

The children for a few moments looked very serious, and each appeared to be inwardly making some kind of promise or resolution to themselves respecting the expected stranger: at length, Ellen, looking up, said to her mamma, with great earnestness—"Indeed, mamma, I will love Miss Hanson as much as if she were my sister, if she will permit me to do it."

"You had better say, Ellen, that you will be as kind to her as if she were your sister; for until we know more of her, it is not possible for us to promise so much; nor is it advisable to give our hearts at first sight, even to those who have yet stronger claims upon our good will and friendly services."

Mr. Harewood added his approbation of this sentiment, for he knew it was one that could not be repeated too often to young people, who are ever apt to take up either partialities or prejudices too strongly, and whose judgment has ever occasion for the attempering lessons of experience.

Mrs. Hofland

CHAPTER II

At length the long-wished-for day arrived, and the young foreigner made her appearance in the family of Mr. Harewood. She was a fine, handsome-looking girl, and though younger in fact, was taller and older-looking than Ellen, but was not nearly so well shaped, as indolence, and the habit of being carried about instead of walking, had occasioned her to stoop, and to move as if her limbs were too weak to support her.

The kindness and politeness with which she was received in the family of Mr. Harewood, did not appear to affect the Barbadoes girl in any other way than to increase that self-importance which was evidently her characteristic; and even the mild, affectionate Ellen, who had predisposed her heart to love her very dearly, shrunk from the proud and haughty expression which frequently animated her features, and was surprised to hear her name her mamma with as much indifference as if she were a common acquaintance; for Ellen did not know that the indulgence of bad passions hardens the heart, and renders it insensible to those sweet and tender ties which are felt by the good and amiable, and which constitute their highest happiness.

In a very short time, it became apparent that passion and peevishness were also the traits of this unfortunate child, who had been indulged in the free exercise of a railing tongue, and even of a clawing hand, towards the numerous negro dependants that swarmed in her father's mansion, over whom she had exercised all the despotic sovereignty of a queen, with the capriciousness of a petted child, and thereby obtained a habit of tyranny over all whom she deemed her inferiors, as appeared from the style in which she now conducted herself constantly towards the menials of Mr. Harewood's family, and not unfrequently towards the superiors.

For a few days Mr. Harewood bore with this conduct, and only opposed it with gentleness and persuasion; but as it became evident that this gentleness emboldened the mistaken child to proceed to greater rudeness, he commenced a new style of treatment, and the English education of Matilda, so far as concerned that most important part of all education, the management of the temper, in the following manner:

On the family being seated at the dinner-table, Miss Hanson called out, in a loud and angry tone, "Give me some beer!"

Mr. Harewood had previously instructed the servant who waited upon them how to act, in case he was thus addressed; and in consequence of his master's commands, the man took no notice whatever of this claim upon his attention.

"Give me some beer!" cried she again, in so fierce a manner that the boys started, and poor Ellen blushed very deeply, not only from the sense of shame which she felt for the vulgarity of the young lady's manners, but from a kind of terror, on hearing such a shrill and threatening voice.

The servant still took no notice of her words, though he did not do it with an air of defiance, but rather as if it were not addressed to him.

The little angry child muttered, loud enough to be heard—"What a fool the wretch is!" but as nobody answered what was in fact addressed to no one, she was at length compelled to look for redress to Mrs. Harewood, whom, regarding with a mixture of rage and scorn, she now addressed—"Pray, ma'am, why don't *you* tell the man to give me some beer? I suppose he'll understand *you*, though he seems a fool, and deaf."

"My children are accustomed to say—'Please, Thomas, give me some beer;' or, 'I'll thank you for a little beer;' and the loud rude manner in which you spoke, probably astonished and confused him. As, however, I certainly understand you, I will endeavour to relieve you.—Pray, Thomas, be so kind as to give Miss Hanson some beer," said Mrs. Harewood.

Thomas instantly offered it; but the little girl cried out in a rage—"I won't have it—no! that I won't, from that man: I'll have my own negro to wait—that I will!—Must I say *please* to a servant? must a nasty man in a livery be *kind* to me?—no! no! no! Zebby, Zebby, I say, come here!"

The poor black woman, hearing the loud tones of her young lady, to which she had been pretty well used, instantly ran into the room, before Mr. Harewood had time to prevent it, and very humbly cried out—"What does Missy please wanty?"

"Some beer, you black beetle!"

"Is, Missy," said the poor woman, with a sigh, reaching the beer from Thomas with a trembling hand, as if she expected the glass to be thrown in her face.

Charles had with great difficulty refrained from laughter on the outset of this scene; but indignation now suffused his countenance. The young vixen was an acute observer, and, had she not been cruelly neglected, might have been a sensible child. It instantly struck her, that his features disputed her right; and, determined not to endure this from any one, she instantly threw the beer in the face of poor Zebby, saying—"There's that for *you*, madam."

It was not in the forbearance of the children to repress their feelings; even Edmund exclaimed—"What a brute!"

Ellen involuntarily started up, and hid her face in her mother's lap, while Charles most good-naturedly offered his handkerchief to the aggrieved Zebby, kindly condoling with her on her misfortune.

Mr. Harewood now, for the first time, spoke.—"Zebby," said he, in a calm but stern tone, "it is my strict command, that so long as you reside under my roof, you never give that young lady any thing again, nor hold any conversation with her: if you disobey my commands, I shall be under the necessity of discharging you."

The young lady checked herself, and for a moment looked alarmed; but recovering, she said—"She is not *yours*, and you sha'n't discharge her: she is my *own* slave, and I will do what I please with her; poor papa bought her for me, as soon as I was born, and I'll use her as I please."

"But you know your mamma told you, that as soon as she arrived in England she would be *free*, and might either return or remain, as *she* pleased. Now it so happens that she is much pleased with my family, and having a sincere regard for your mother, she this morning requested Mrs. Harewood to engage her in any service she could undertake: convinced that she was worthy our protection, we have done this, and therefore all *your* claims upon her are over."

The little girl, bursting into a passionate flood of tears, ran out of the room.

Poor Zebby, courtesying, said—"Sir, me hopes you will have much pity on Missy—she was spoily all her life, by poor massa—her mamma good, very good; and when Missy pinch Zebby, and pricky with pin, then good mississ she be angry; but massa say only—'Poo! poo! she be child—naughty tricks wear off in time.' He be warm man himself."

The poor negro's defence affected the little circle, and Mr. Harewood observing it, said—"You perceive, my dear children, that this child is in fact far more an object of compassion than blame, for she has been permitted to indulge every bad propensity of her nature, and their growth has destroyed that which was good; of course, her life has been unhappy in itself, yet punishment has not produced amendment. Poor thing! how many of the sweetest pleasures of existence are unknown to her! She is a stranger to the satisfaction of obliging others, and to the consciousness of overcoming herself, which, I trust, you all know to be an inestimable blessing. I truly pity her; but I am compelled to treat her as if I blamed her only; I am obliged to be harsh, in order that I may be useful, and give pain to produce ease."

In about an hour, finding that no one approached, and feeling the want of the dinner her shameful rudeness and petulance had interrupted, and which she had but just begun, Matilda came down stairs, with the air of a person who is struggling to hide, by effrontery, the chagrin she is conscious of deserving: no person took any notice of her entrance, and all appearance of the good meal she wanted was removed. There was a certain something in the usually-smiling faces of the heads of the mansion that acted as a repellent to her, and she sat for some time silent; but at length she spoke to Ellen, who, from her gentle meekness, was ever easy of access, and whom, intending to mortify, she accosted thus—"Nelly, did you eat my chicken?"

Charles burst into a loud laugh, as Ellen, who had never heard herself thus addressed, for a moment looked rather foolish; on which he answered for her, with a somewhat provoking sauciness of countenance—"No, Matty, she did not eat your chicken."

"My name is not Matty—it is Matilda Sophia, and you are a great booby for calling me so; but Nelly, or Nell, is short for Ellen, and by one of those names I shall call her, whenever I choose, if it be only to vex *you*."

"Perhaps, too, you will choose to prick her, and pinch her, Miss Matilda Sophia Hanson?" answered Charles, sneeringly, drawing out her name as long and as pompously as it was possible.

"Fie, Charles!" said Edmund; "I am sure you act as if you had forgotten all that papa told us about Miss Hanson."

Charles, after a moment's thought, acknowledged that he was wrong, very, very wrong.

Matilda was much struck with this; she was well aware that, under the same circumstances, she should have said much more than he had, and she was curious as to what had been said of her, which could have produced this effect on a boy generally so vivacious and warm-tempered as Charles. After cogitating upon it some time, she at length concluded that Mr. Harewood had endeavoured to impress on the minds of his family the consequence she possessed, as an only child and a great heiress; and although he had appeared so lately to act under a very different impression, yet it was very possible that he had only done so because he was out of

Mrs. Hofland

temper himself, and, now his mind was become tranquil again, he had repented of his conduct, and been anxious to prevent his children from following his example in this respect.

The more Matilda thought of this, the more fully she fixed it in her mind as an article of belief; but yet there was something in the calm, firm tones of Mr. Harewood, when he spoke to her, and in his present open, yet unbending countenance, when he happened to cast his eyes towards her, which rendered her unsatisfied with the answer she thus gave her own internal inquiries; and although she had been exceedingly angry with him, for presuming to speak to her, she yet felt as if his esteem, and indeed his forgiveness, were necessary for her happiness; and her pride, thus strengthened, contended with her fears and consciousness of guilt and folly; and while she resolved inwardly to keep up her dignity with the young ones, she yet, from time to time, cast an anxious eye towards her new monitor.

In a short time, to Matilda's great relief, Mr. Harewood stepped into the library to get a book; and the children, in the hope that, when he returned, he would kindly indulge them, either by reading to them, or relating occasionally such anecdotes or observations as the work he read might furnish him with, left their seats, and pressed round the place where their parents were sitting.

Matilda did not like to be left alone, nor did she feel as if she had a right to be held as a child among the rest: again her pride and her repentance had a great struggle, and she knew not to which she should give the preference, for her heart swelled alike with pride and sorrow; she moved towards the same place, and sought, in the bustle of the moment, to divert the painful feeling which oppressed her.

In a few moments, Mr. Harewood was heard to shut the library-door; and as, of course, he might be expected to re-enter very soon, and would now be much nearer to her than he had been, and would certainly adopt some more decided kind of conduct and language towards her, Matilda became again extremely desirous of knowing what he really had said about her, and she two or three times essayed to speak; but a little remaining modesty, which was nearly all the good which her unhappy education had left her, prevented her, until she found that she had no time beyond the present instant left for satisfying her curiosity on so important a point, when, in a considerable flutter of spirits, she whispered to Ellen, but in a voice sufficiently articulate to be heard by others—"Pray what did your papa say of me?"

"That you were very much to be pitied."

"Pitied! Pray what am I to be pitied for?"

Ellen blushed very deeply: she could not answer a question which called down confusion on the head of her who asked it—one, too, whom she was inclined to love, and whose petulance towards herself, however unprovoked, she had already forgiven. She looked wistfully in the face of her mamma, who replied for her—"We all think you are much to be pitied, because you are evidently a poor, little, forlorn, ignorant child, without friends, and under the dominion of a cruel enemy, that renders you so frightful, it is scarcely possible for even the most humane people to treat you with kindness, or even endure you."

Matilda involuntarily started up, and examined herself in the looking-glass.—"If I had happened to be your *own* daughter, ma'am," she said, crying again, "you would not have thought me ugly; but because I come from Barbadoes, you don't like me; and it is cruel and wicked to treat me so.

But I will go back—I will—I will."

"I wish most sincerely you had never come, for it is painful to me to witness the folly and sin you are guilty of; but, since you are here, I will endeavour to bear with you, until I have found a good school to send you to. If you would give yourself time to consider, you would know that the enemy I spoke of is your own temper, which would render even perfect beauty hideous; you know very well that I received you with the greatest kindness, and that you have outraged that kindness. But I can forgive you, because I see that you are a silly child, who fancies herself of importance; whereas children, however they may be situated, are poor dependent creatures."

Matilda answered only by a scornful toss of her head, and uttering the word—"Dependent!"

"Edmund," said Mrs. Harewood, taking no notice of her insolent look, "you are a strong healthy boy, forward in your education, capable of reflection, and decidedly superior, not only in age, but wisdom, to any other in the room; answer me candidly, as if you were speaking to a boy like yourself—Do you feel it possible so to conduct yourself, that, if you were left alone in the world, you could be happy and independent?"

"My dear mamma," said Edmund, "you must be laughing at me; a pretty figure I should cut, if I were to set up for a man, without any one to advise me how to act, to tell me when I was wrong, and to manage every thing for me! how could I do right without my papa, or some proper guardian? and how could I be happy without you, mamma?"

As Edmund spoke, he threw his arms round his mother; and the others followed his example, saying—"No, no, we could do nothing without you and dear papa; pray do stay with us, and make us good."

As they spoke, the tears were in their eyes, and Matilda was affected: she remembered the tenderness of her own mother, and how often she had turned a deaf ear to her expostulations. She was convinced that these children, at this very time, enjoyed a sweeter pleasure than she had ever experienced from the gratification of her desires, and she even longed to confess her folly, and gain her share of Mrs. Harewood's caresses; but pride still struggled in her heart; and though her reason was convinced of the truth, that children are indeed dependent on their friends for all that renders life valuable, yet her temper still got the better, and she resolutely held her tongue, though she ceased to look haughty and ill-humoured.

CHAPTER III

This interesting display of natural feelings was interrupted by the hasty re-entrance of Mr. Harewood, followed by Betty, the housemaid, who, in entering the door in a hurry, had fallen down a step, and hurt her forehead, and was now brought forward by her good master, to claim the assistance of her kind and skilful mistress.

The children were full of concern and condolence with Betty, and with great tenderness shrunk when they saw their mamma bathe her forehead with vinegar, as they knew it must smart exceedingly: and Ellen could not help saying—"How good Betty is! she never says oh!"

"No, Miss," said Betty, "I know your mamma does it for my good; and though she gives me some pain, yet she saves me from a great deal more."

In a few minutes, Betty declared the smarting was quite gone; and the children were so glad, that Matilda began to think, though they were foolish, yet they were certainly happy, and she wished she could feel as happy as they did.

When Betty was gone, the tea came in, and Mrs. Harewood ordered a large plate of toast, as she recollected Matilda's scanty dinner. Thomas once handed it all round, and Mr.

Harewood then said—"Set it down; when the children want it, they will ask you for it."

All the children remembered poor Matilda's wants, and in order that she might have plenty, without any more being ordered, or any thing in reference to the past being mentioned, with true delicacy of feeling, forbore to eat any more, so that Matilda could not repeat their words in asking, which she now determined to do. She was very hungry, and the toast looked very tempting, as it stood before the fire.

Matilda looked at the toast, and then at the footman; her cheek glowed, her eye was subdued, but her tongue did not move. Thomas, however, handed her the toast, and she then articulately said—"Thank you."

This was heard, but no notice was taken; they knew that much false shame attends the first efforts to subdue pride and passion, and they feared lest even approbation should be misconstrued.

In order to divert the general attention, Mrs. Harewood said—"I forgot to ask Betty what made her run in such a hurry as to occasion her accident, for I gave her leave to go out, and stay till nine o'clock, and it is only seven now, I believe."

"I believe, madam," said Thomas, very respectfully, "she came home in haste, because her sister has twins; and as you promised her some caudle, she came to tell the cook to make it, and likewise to get some little matter of clothing, from her own clothes, for the baby that is unprovided."

"Poor woman!" said Mrs. Harewood; "we must all help; this little stranger has a claim on us."

Ellen clapped her hands—"Oh, mamma, may I make it a nightcap?"

"Yes, my dear; I will get some old linen, and cut out a few things, after tea."

"I will give you a crown, my dear," said Mr. Harewood; "as I cannot assist in sewing, I must help to buy needles and thread."

"And I will give you a shilling, mamma," said Edmund, "if you please."

"Oh dear," said Charles, "I am very sorry, but I have only fourpence, because I spent all my money on my new kite; but if that will do any good, mamma—"

"It will do good, Charles, and I will not grieve you by refusing it, because I see you are sorry that you have no more, which will teach you another time to be provident, and then you will not be under the necessity of giving your last farthing, or refusing to be charitable, when such a case occurs again."

Ellen handed Charles's fourpence to her mamma; and as she did so, she put a sixpence between the pence, so as not to be seen by Matilda, lest it should seem like a reproach to her; and as she slipped the whole into her mother's hand, she said—"I hope, mamma, you will be so good as to let Miss Hanson make a little cap for the baby?"

"I don't like to sew," said Matilda, rising; "at least not such things as these: I think a bit of calico to wrap the pick-aninnies in is the best, and I'll give that to buy some with."

As she spoke she threw half-a-guinea on the table, with the

air of one desirous of exhibiting both generosity and wealth, and looked round with an eye that asked for admiration.

No notice was taken. Mrs. Harewood opening her own purse, took out half-a-crown, and then counted all that she had got. In doing it, Ellen perceived not her sixpence, and she then, with modesty, but without any shame, said—"I believe my sixpence must have slipped down."

"I did not know you gave me one, child."

"Yes, but she did, for I saw her," said Mr. Harewood, "though she was not aware that I did. She gave it in silence, not from affectation, but a kind motive towards one who could not appreciate it; but we will say no more on this point. Ellen, you have gratified your father: I see in your conduct the germ of a gentlewoman, and, what is infinitely more precious, of a Christian."

Ellen sprung to her father's arms, and in his affectionate kiss found a rich reward.

For a moment, Matilda thought to herself, what a piece of work is here about sixpence, while they take no notice at all of a bright golden half-guinea! but still her understanding combated this thought, for she knew that all the present company saw beyond the surface, and estimated the gift according to the spirit of the donor.

Betty now came in, and Mrs. Harewood gave her the money, telling her to buy some frocks with it. Observing the servant eye the half-guinea, she said—"*That* was the gift of Miss Hanson; she is very rich, it seems, and gives out of her abundance. I am sure you will be grateful to *her*; but if your fellow-servants, Betty, should spare, out of the little time they have, enough to assist you in the making of these things, they will be the best friends you meet with; for labour is much greater charity than money."

Betty replied, that she was much obliged to all her friends, both above and below, and especially to poor Zebby, who had offered, with her lady's leave, to sit up all night with her sister.

"She has not only my leave, but my approbation, especially as your accident has rendered you unable. Tell Zebby I will spare her for a week, on this truly charitable occasion."

With many thanks, Betty withdrew, and Ellen was soon, like her mamma, busy with her needle. Mr. Harewood, drawing a celestial globe towards him, began to give his sons some instruction, which interested them exceedingly; all were employed, all happy, but Matilda, whose uneasiness was in fact considerably augmented by the idea of Zebby leaving the house; for though she used her ill, she had a regard for her, the extent of which she was not aware of till now that her heart was a little softened, and her judgment enlightened, by the transactions of the day.

After fidgeting about for some time, she at length took up a needle and threaded it, and then drawing more timidly towards Mrs. Harewood, she said—"I don't mind if I do sew a little bit."

Eager to seize upon any good symptom, Mrs. Harewood gave her a little cap, carefully doubled down, saying—"You see this is double; in these countries, the babies, or pickaninnies, as you call them, must be kept warm."

"I called that woman's twins pickaninnies, because I thought she was poor—a kind of servant; we do not call white children so—only little negroes."

"They are all the same with us, and will be so with you, I hope, by and by; indeed they always were with sensible good people. But, Matilda, what long stitches you are taking! I shall have all your work to pick out again."

"I believe I cannot sew, indeed."

"So it appears; nor can you play a tune, nor read a French lesson, nor write, nor draw: poor little girl! you have a great deal to learn: but, however, keep up your spirits; if you are diligent and tractable, you will conquer all your difficulties; humility and industry will enable you to learn every thing."

"How very strange it is," said Matilda to herself, "that these people appear to pity me, instead of envying me, as they used to do in Barbadoes, and as I thought they would do here! besides, they are not angry with me, even when they find fault with me, and they seem to wish me to be good for the sake of being happy."

These thoughts somewhat soothed the perturbed bosom of the poor child until the hour of rest, when the remembrance of the good-tempered negro's destination rose to her mind, and she lamented her absence, and blamed her exceedingly for leaving *her* to go after a woman she had never seen in her life: but the next day, it was apparent that the lesson she had received was not lost upon her; she appeared ashamed of her ignorance, and willing to learn; and as all her young friends were very willing to instruct her, in whatever they had the power, she soon began to make some progress in her education; she was a child of good capacity, and, when roused to exertion, unusually quick; and being at an age when the mind expands quickly, it was no wonder that she soon gave evident marks of improvement. It was observed, that as her mind became enlightened, her manners were softened, and her petulance less obtrusive, though she was

Mrs. Hofland

seen to suffer daily from the habitual violence of her temper, and the disposition to insolence, which unchecked power is so apt to foster in young minds.

Mrs. Harewood found the care of Matilda greatly increase her task of managing her family, as one naughty child frequently makes another, by raising up a spirit of contention and ill-humour; and Charles was so frequently led into sallies of passion, or tempted to ridicule the fault in his new companion, that his parents often lamented that they had accepted such a burdensome charge: but when they saw any symptoms of improvement in her, they were ever happy to foster the good seed; and in the consciousness that they were not only raising up a human mind to virtue and happiness, but preparing an immortal soul for heaven, they thought little of their own trouble, and were even truly thankful that she had been intrusted to their careful examination and affectionate discipline.

CHAPTER IV

At the end of the week, Zebby came home, according to appointment; and having paid her respects to her excellent lady, she ran up stairs, and entered the apartment where the two young ladies were getting the tasks assigned them by Mrs. Harewood. When Matilda first beheld her she had a great inclination to embrace her, for her heart bounded towards the only creature she had been acquainted with from her cradle; but she suddenly checked herself, and pretended to continue her reading; but Ellen spoke to her kindly, though she told her that she was so situated, as not to be able to chat at present.

Zebby comprehended this, and would have withdrawn; but not to have a single word from her, whom in her heart, she still considered as her young mistress, the faithful creature could not endure; after waiting some minutes in vain, she dropped a second humble courtesy, and said—"How you do, Missy? me very glad see you larn booky, but me hopes you spare one look, one wordy, for poor Zebby; me go away one long weeky, to nurse white man baby, pretty as you, Missy."

"Yes," said Matilda, reproachingly, "you went away and left me very willingly, though it was to wait on a person you never saw before."

Mrs. Hofland

"Ah, Missy! you no lovee me, and poor white woman lovee me much. You makee beer spit in my face—she givee me tea-gruel out of her own cup. You callee me black beetle—she callee me good girly, good nursy, good every ting."

Matilda gave a deep sigh; she well remembered that it was on the very day of her outrage that Zebby had quitted her, and in her altered sense of justice, she could not help seeing the truth of the poor negro's statement; she looked up, with an ingenuous sense of error depicted on her countenance, and said—"I am sorry, Zebby, that I used you so ill, but I will never do it again."

The poor African was absolutely astonished, for never had the voice of concession been heard from the lips of Matilda before, even to her own parents; and the idea of her humility and kindness in this acknowledgment so deeply affected the faithful creature, that, after gazing at her in admiration for a moment, she burst into tears, and then clasping her hands, she exclaimed, in a broken manner—"Oh, tankee God! tankee God! pretty Missy be good girly at last! her lovee her good mamma—her pity poor negro—her go up stair when her die. Oh, me be so glad! great God lovee my dear Missy now!"

Matilda felt the tears suffuse her own eyes, as the kind heart of her late faithful slave thus gave vent to its natural and devout emotions; and she gave her hand to Zebby, who kissed it twenty times. Ellen was so delighted with this proof of good disposition in Matilda, and with the honest effusions of the poor negro, that she could not forbear gratifying her own affectionate little heart, by running to tell her dear mamma, who truly rejoiced in every proof of Matilda's amendment, and doubted not but it would prove the forerunner of virtue, in a child who appeared convinced of her faults, and desirous of improving herself.

It was now near Christmas, and Mrs. Harewood was inquiring for a boarding-school where she could place Miss Hanson. She would have preferred to keep her at home, and have a governess, who might attend to the instructions necessary both for her and Ellen; but the bad temper and insolent airs of Matilda had prevented this, as Mrs. Harewood could not bear the idea of subjecting an amiable young person, whom she designed for that situation, to be tormented with such a girl. She knew that, in schools, two faults seldom fail to be cured: these are impertinence, or insolence, and affectation—one rendering a person disagreeable, the other ridiculous; and every member in the community of which a school consists, is ready to assist the ruler in punishing the one, and laughing at the other.

One morning, when Matilda got out of bed, she went to look whether the morning was fine, and the moment she got to the window, eagerly cried out, in great surprise—"Ellen, Ellen! get up this moment, and come to the window; the whole world is covered with white! and see, there are thousands and thousands of little white feathers coming from the skies, as if the angels were emptying feather-beds upon the earth."

"It snows," said Ellen, calmly; "I recollect my papa told us you had never seen it snow."

"What is snow?"

"We will ask Edmund; he can tell you much better than I can."

The surprising appearance thus witnessed, induced Matilda to hasten down stairs, where Edmund was writing his Latin exercise.—"Do pray tell me," she cried, "what snow is, and why I never saw it before?"

Mrs. Hofland

"Snow," said Edmund, "is nothing but drops of rain, which, in passing through the cold air, become congealed or frozen. If you take this pretty light substance into your warm hand, it will melt and become a rain-drop again."

As Edmund spoke, he opened the window a very little way, caught some snow, and showed her the effect he spoke of.

"But why did I never see this in Barbadoes?"

"Because Barbadoes lies nearer to the sun than England, and is much warmer, even in winter; therefore the rain-drops never pass through that region of cold air which freezes them in northern climates. If you were to go farther north, you would find still more snow and ice, the same I saw you looking at yesterday. I will lend you a little book, where you will see a description of a palace of ice, and of whole mountains of snow, called Glaciers; and, if you please, I will show you that part of the globe, or earth, in which those effects begin to take place. But, my dear Ellen, pray lend Matilda your tippet, for she looks as much frozen as the snow; she must take great care of herself in this cold climate."

Ellen threw the pinafore she was going to put on over the neck of the shuddering Matilda, and then ran nimbly before them towards the globe, on which Edmund was going to lecture, neither of them looking in Matilda's face; but Charles, who just then happened to enter, perceived that silent tears were coursing each other down her cheek. His compassion was moved; he apprehended that the cold, which he felt himself to be severe, had made her ill, and he inquired what was the matter with her, in a tone of real commiseration.

"I am so—so very ignorant," said Matilda, sobbing.

"Oh, that's it!" cried Charles, gaily; "then you and I may shake hands, for I am ignorant too."

"Oh no, European children know every thing, but I am little better than a negro; I find what your mamma said was very true—I know nothing at all."

"Dear Matilda, how can you say so?" said Edmund; "though you have not read as much as we have, yet you have seen a great deal more than any of us, and you are the youngest of the company, you know. Consider, you have crossed the Atlantic Ocean, seen groves of orange-trees and spices grow, and the whole process of sugar-making. You know the inside of a ship as well as a house, and we never saw any thing better than a sloop, or sailed any where but on the Thames."

"Besides," said Charles, "you have seen monkeys and parrots, and many other creatures, in their own country, and many curious fish on your voyage. Oh, you understand natural history much better than we do."

"And if you understand nothing at all," added Ellen, kindly pressing her hand, "mamma says it is only *wilful* ignorance that is blameable."

Matilda wept still more while the children thus tried to comfort her. This distressed them all; but they rejoiced to see their parents enter the room, persuaded that they would be able to comfort her better, and Ellen instantly besought their attention to the subject by relating as much of the foregoing conversation as was necessary.

"No, no, it is not exactly *that* I am crying for," said Matilda, interrupting her; "it is because I have been so very naughty, and you are all so—so—so—"

"So what, my dear?" said Mr. Harewood, drawing her towards him, and placing her by his side, in the same manner he was accustomed to let Ellen stand, when she was much in his favour.

The action, however kindly meant, for a time redoubled her tears; and the children, understanding their mamma's look, withdrew to the room where they usually breakfasted, without the least symptom of discontent, although they perceived their mamma fill a cup of tea for Matilda at her own table.

When they were gone, and the little girl had somewhat recovered, Mr. Harewood whispered her—"Did you mean to say, my dear, that my children were so clever, or so proud, or so what?"

"Oh, sir, they are so *good*! that was what I wanted to say; for there was Edmund who always looked so grave, and was poring over his books, he talked to me quite kindly, and never made the least game of me, for all I must look like a fool in his eyes, who has seen the snow all his life. And then Charles, who is so full of fun and nonsense, and who I always thought could not abide me, he spoke to me as if he was sorry for me, and made it out that we were both ignorant alike; and when I remembered how I had looked at them, and behaved to them, I felt as if my heart would break. Ellen is always so good, that I did not think so much of her kindness, but nobody knows—"

Again the repentant girl wept, and at length with difficulty proceeded—"Nobody knows how dearly I love her, and *you* too."

She received the kindest assurances from both Mr. and Mrs. Harewood of their affection, and that they fully believed she would conquer her bad temper, now she saw how much it was not only her duty, but happiness to do so; and Mr. Harewood assured her that he had no doubt, but in the course of a few years, he should see her as sensible, good, and well-informed, as his own children.

"And then I shall not be an object of pity, sir?"

"No, you will be one of affection and esteem."

"Oh, I doubt that must never, *never* be!"

"Never despair; though you have many battles with yourself, yet never relinquish the hope of final conquest, and be assured you will find every victory easier than the last. When you find pride rising in your heart, think on your ignorance, and it will make you humble; and when you are inclined to be angry with those around you, remember what you have this day confessed respecting their kindness, and it will make you bear with the present vexation; and if at any time you are discomfited in any pursuit, either of virtue or knowledge, recollect what I now say, that, with many faults, yet you have some merit, and may therefore reasonably hope to attain more."

"Have I indeed?" said the now-humbled girl.

"Yes, you have an inquiring mind, which is one great step towards the attainment of knowledge, and you are sincere and open-hearted, which enables your friends to see what is the real bent of your disposition, and to give you the advice really necessary; and I hope, with this groundwork of good, you will be a very different girl when your mother again sees you."

Mr. Harewood left Matilda quieted, but deeply impressed by what he had said.

CHAPTER V

From this time, Matilda felt as if her heart was lightened of a heavy load, and she looked up to Mr. and Mrs. Harewood as friends, whom it was her duty to obey and her privilege to love; and to the children, as brothers, whose pleasures were as dear to her as her own; and the warmth and openness of her temper naturally led her to display more than usual friendship, wherever she professed it at all. Happily, with all her faults, she was neither mean, artful, nor deceitful; so that the worst part of her disposition lay open to the observation of those good friends, who, like skilful physicians, only wounded to cure her.

The errors of Matilda were those which never fail to attach to extreme indulgence—pride, impetuosity, haughtiness, inso-lence, and idleness. Accustomed to consider all around her as born for her use and amusement, she commanded where she should have entreated, and resisted where she ought to have obeyed; but when she found that her wealth, power, and consequence were unknown, or utterly disregarded, and that she could only be esteemed for her good qualities, even her self-love tended to cure her of her idleness; and instead of drawling out—"Zebby, bring me this," "You fool, fetch me the other," she administered to her own wants, and obtained her wishes at so much less expense than she had once thought possible, that even her own convenience taught her the wisdom of waiting upon herself. She imputed the change, which could not fail to be remarked, to the climate—and unquestionably it is more easy and pleasant to be active in a cold country, than a hot one; but her friends were well aware that the change in her mind was greater than that of her country, and they forwarded this happy effect, by rendering the studies in which she engaged as delightful to her as possible, in order that, by prosecuting them, she might become less liable to rest her happiness on the vain pomp, useless show, and tyrannical power, which were wont to delight her.

As, however, all bad habits are slowly eradicated, and it by no means follows that even the error we have lamented and acknowledged should be so torn from the heart that no traces remain, so it would happen, from time to time, that Matilda would fly into violent passions with the servants around her, as with her young companions; and even when these were suppressed, she was apt to give herself airs of importance, and descant on the privileges she enjoyed in her own country, where she was fanned when she was hot, by slaves upon their knees, and borne about in a stately palanquin; where the most exquisite fruits were continually presented to court her palate, and the most costly dresses that money could procure purchased to please her; where every slave trembled at her anger, or rejoiced in her smile; and where she would one day return to reign as absolute as an empress.

"Well," said Ellen, one night, as this conversation took place in the play-room, "I must own I should like to live at Barbadoes for one thing—I should like to set all the slaves at liberty, and dress their little children, and make all happy; as to all the other *good* things and *grand* things, I really think we have quite sufficient of them at home; for I suppose there are no more books nor charities in your country than ours, Matilda; and surely there can be no greater pleasure in this world, than reading the 'Parent's Assistant,' and giving clothes and food to poor children when they are really hungry and starving?"

"Certainly not," cried Charles; "depend upon it, Ellen, England is the finest land in the world; and though I should like to see oranges and pine-apples grow, I confess, and the poor slaves at their merry meeting, all dancing away, with their woolly heads and white teeth, as happy as princes, yet, depend upon it, there is nothing else half so beautiful as with us. England is unquestionably the most beautiful, excellent, rich, delightful country upon the globe."

As Charles spoke, he fixed his eyes upon Edmund; for although the ardour of his spirits rendered him a great dealer in positive assertions, he was yet so conscious of his inferiority in knowledge to his eldest brother, that he seldom felt satisfied with them, unless they were stamped by his brother's approbation.

Edmund, in answer to his appealing eye, said—"I am as well convinced as you can be, Charles, that England combines more advantages than any other country, and that we either have in ourselves, or obtain from other countries, whatever is most worthy of possession; and the two good things which Ellen considers the greatest pleasures of existence, are undoubtedly to be had here in perfection; but I must own I should like to see Barbadoes prodigiously, for a property which none of you have yet mentioned."

"What, have not *I* mentioned it?" said Matilda.

"No, Matilda; you have been so much taken up with fine verandas, grand dinners, kneeling slaves, luxurious palan-quins, orange groves, and delicious sweetmeats, that you have never once boasted of your pure air, and the glories of your evening sky, where all the planets shine with such a glowing lustre, that, Mr. Edwards tells us, Venus is there a kind of moon, in the light she sheds upon the earth, and those stars which are scarcely to be discerned here, are beheld in that enchanting air as bright as the stars of Orion with us."

"Well," cried Charles, "that must all be because Barbadoes, and the other West India islands, are so much nearer the sun, and I cannot say I have any desire to be in such a hot neighbourhood."

"No, Charles, that is not the reason; for although it is the fact, yet you cannot suppose that their difference can be perceptible, in that respect, to those heavenly bodies which appear to resemble only diamond sparks, from their immense distance. The brilliancy of which I speak arises from the greater purity of the air: we frequently see objects here through a kind of veil, which, though too thin to be perceptible, has yet its effect upon all objects: in some cases it alters, or rather bestows, a colour which does not properly belong to them; frequently impairs their form and beauty, but sometimes adds to their sublimity, and invests them with imposing greatness, proportioned to the obscurity with which they are enveloped."

"I don't understand all that Edmund says," observed Ellen, "but I should be glad to know whether something is not the matter with the sun when it looks copper-colour like the lid of a stewpan; because in summer-time, I remember, when we were out in the fields, it used to be bright golden yellow, so glorious and full of shine, as it were, that looking at it, even for a moment, made my eyes ache, and thousands of black and green spots to come into them."

"My dear Ellen, though you did not understand all the words I used, it is yet plain you did comprehend the sense, as you have brought forward an example of this effect of the atmosphere, which we all witness every day; the fogs and exhalations through which we view the sun are the cause of that dingy appearance you remark: and even in the summer-time, as the sun descends, you may perceive he becomes more and more red and dark as he approaches the horizon. I have therefore no doubt but the veil, or vapoury substance, of which I speak, is but a little distance from the earth; for I observe, that as the sun rises into the heavens, he grows more brilliant from surmounting this veil."

"Did you find this out of yourself, Edmund?"

"I noticed it one day to papa, and he explained it; he told me, too, that all the beautiful variety of colours which we observe in the setting sun must be imputed to this cause; he taught me at the same time to distinguish shadows in the water by reflection, and those which are refracted, and many other things, which rendered me much more delighted with the country than I had ever been before, and more fond of dear papa for taking the trouble to inform me."

"Well then," said Ellen, "when we go down to Richmond next summer, you must explain every thing to us, and we will love you better than ever, dear Edmund; and I will say the Ode to Eton College to you in my very best manner; perhaps Matilda will be able to say it before then, and—"

"Go on, Ellen."

"I want to know—*we* want to know what it means in that poem, where it says,

    'Grateful Science still adores
    Her Henry's holy shade.'

What is a holy shade, Edmund?"

"It is a poetical expression, my dear, meaning that we of the present day are grateful to the founder, Henry the Sixth, who was a religious, and probably a learned man, although very unfortunate as a king."

"Oh," cried Ellen, "I remember all about him; he was deposed by Edward the Fourth, whose two sons were afterwards murdered in the Tower by their wicked uncle, Richard the Third."

"I remember *that*," said Matilda, timidly, yet with that kind of pleasure which indicated a sense of approaching her superior in knowledge, and being sensible that this was the only kind of superiority worth possessing.

Scarcely, however, had she spoken, when Charles, throwing himself into a theatrical attitude, exclaimed—"Ay! but do you remember the man that looked like *him*—to this same Henry, *'Who drew Priam's curtains in the dead of night, and would have told him half his Troy was burnt?'*"

"No, indeed," said both the girls, staring.

Charles burst into a loud laugh at their innocent surprise at his violent gesticulation and grimace.

"I know what you mean," said Ellen, rather poutingly; "yes, I know it very well, though I don't choose to talk about things of that kind, because I have always been told that none but ignorant and foolish people did so."

"But I entreat you," said Charles, "to tell me what you think I mean, for I am sure you surprise me now as much as I did you."

Mrs. Hofland

"Why, I suppose Henry's holy shade means spirit, and it was that which drew Priam's curtains in the dead of night, (or which he thought did,) though it was probably only the housemaid."

Again Charles burst into an immoderate fit of laughter, exclaiming—"Housemaid! admirable! upon my word, Ellen, you have found a personage in the old king's establishment Homer never thought of."

"I never read Homer," said Ellen, simply.

"No, child, you need not tell us that," continued Charles, most provokingly continuing to laugh, until poor Ellen was completely disconcerted, and looked in the face of Edmund with such an appealing air, that he assumed a look of much more serious remonstrance than was usual as he thus addressed his brother—"You may laugh as long as you please, sir, but your whole conduct in this affair has shown so much less knowledge, as well as good sense, than Ellen herself has displayed, that really I should not wonder if a moment's recollection made you cry as heartily as you now laugh."

"Indeed!" said Charles, suddenly stopping.

"Yes, *indeed*! In the first place, there can be surely no doubt but you and I have read a great deal more than the girls, and could at any time puzzle and distress them by various quotations; but when they make inquiries to increase their own stock of knowledge, it is our duty, and ought to be our pleasure, to give them information, not confusion, which you evidently intended to do; besides, it is rude, almost inhuman, to oppress any person, even by the possession of that which is in itself praiseworthy; and as the end of all conversation is, or ought to be, improvement, a person who in any manner checks the spirit of inquiry and free discussion, hinders that end. We all know that English history is all that Ellen has dipped into, and in the little she presumed to utter on the subject, she was perfectly correct; whereas you, in your exhibition of more reading, made a palpable error, since Homer names maids repeatedly as belonging to the palace, and we cannot doubt their being employed as our house-maids are, since their offices are often particularized."

"A mighty piece of work, truly," said Charles, "for just quoting two lines of Shakspeare!"

"No, no, Charles, 'tis not for the quotation, but the manner, and you cannot but see yourself how erroneous an idea was taken up in consequence; how often does papa say people can never be too plain and simple, too downright and unequivocal, in their explanations to children, otherwise they plant words rather than ideas in their minds, and create a confusion which it may take many a year of after-thought to unravel?"

"I was very foolish," said Charles, looking at Ellen with the air of one that wondered how it had been possible to give pain to that little gentle heart, which sought only to bestow pleasure on all around it. He was about to speak, but before he had time, his fond sister had read his heart, and throwing her arms around his neck, she exclaimed—"I know you meant nothing, dear Charles; no, I know you didn't; only you are so fond of being funny."

The eyes of Charles did indeed now twinkle with a tear; and Matilda, who was quick to discern, and acute in all her feelings, was much affected. When they retired, she revolved all the conversation in her mind; she saw clearly that virtue and knowledge were the only passports to happiness; and the remembrance of her mother's desire to teach her various things, which she had either shunned from idleness, or rejected with insolence and ill-humour, rose to her mind; and the unhappy indulgence of her father appeared to her in far different colours to what she had ever beheld it. She became frequently disturbed, and full of painful reflection; yet she evidently took much pains in attaining knowledge of the task assigned her, and in conquering those risings of temper which were become inherent in her mind. Notwithstanding her frequent fits of abstraction, in which it was evident some great grief was uppermost in her mind, yet, as her nature led her to be communicative, and she was never subject to be sullen, the family did not press her to reveal her trouble, thinking that at the proper time she would repose confidence in them; and accordingly, as she sat one day alone with Mrs. Harewood, the following conversation took place between them.

CHAPTER VI

Matilda, after a long silence, in which she was endeavouring, but in vain, to arrange her ideas and calm the incessant beating of her heart, said, timidly and abruptly, with her eyes fixed on the carpet—"Do you think, ma'am, that if Ellen had ever been very, *very* naughty and saucy to *you*, who are so good to *her*, that you could ever really in your heart forgive her?"

"I certainly should consider it my duty to punish her for her disobedience, by withholding my usual expressions of love and my general indulgences from her; but I should undoubtedly forgive her, because, in the first place, God has commanded me to forgive all trespasses, and in the second, my heart would be drawn naturally towards my own child."

"But surely, dear Mrs. Harewood, it is worse for an *own* child to behave ill to a parent than any other person?"

"Undoubtedly, my dear, for it unites the crime of ingratitude to that of disobedience; besides, it is cruel and unnatural to be guilty of insolence and hard-heartedness towards the hand which has reared and fostered us all our lives—which has loved us in despite of our faults—watched over our infancy —instructed our childhood—nursed us in sickness, and prayed for us before we could pray for ourselves."

"My mamma has done all this for me a thousand times," cried Matilda, bursting into tears of bitter contrition, which, for some time, Mrs. Harewood suffered to flow unrestrained; at length she checked herself, but it was only to vent her sorrow by self-accusation—"Oh, ma'am! you cannot think how very ill I have behaved to my dear, dear mother—I have been saucy to her, and bad to every body about me; many a time have I vexed her on purpose; and when she scolded me, I was so pert and disobedient—you can form no idea how bad I was. If she spoke ever so gently to me, I used to tell my papa she had been scolding me, and then he would blame her and justify me; and many a time I have heard deep sighs, that seemed to come from the very bottom of her heart, and the tears would stand in her sweet eyes as she looked at me. Oh, wicked, wicked child that I was, to grieve such a good mamma! and now we are parted such a long, long way, and I cannot beg her pardon—I cannot show her that I am trying to be good; perhaps she may die, as poor papa did, and I shall never, *never* see her more."

The agonies of the repentant girl, as this afflictive thought came over her mind, arose to desperation; and Mrs. Harewood, who felt much for her, endeavoured to bestow some comfort upon her; but poor Matilda, who was ever violent, even in her better feelings, could not, for a long time, listen to the kind voice of her consoler—she could only repeat her own faults, recapitulate all the crimes she had been guilty of, and display, in all their native hideousness, such traits of ill-humour, petulance, ungovernable fury, outrageous passion, and vile revenge, as are the natural offspring of the human heart, when its bad propensities are matured by indulgence, particularly in those warm countries, where the mind partakes the nature of the soil, and slavery in one race of beings gives power to all the bad passions of another.

At length the storm of anguish so far gave way, that Mrs.

Harewood was able to command her attention, and she seized this precious season of penitence and humility to imprint the leading truths of Christianity, and those plain and invaluable doctrines which are deducible from them, and evident to the capacity of any sensible child, without leading from the more immediate object of her anxiety; as Mrs. Harewood very justly concluded, that if she saw her error as a child, and could be brought to conquer her faults as such, it would include every virtue to be expected at her time of life, and would lay the foundation of all those which we estimate in the female character.

"Oh," cried Matilda, sobbing, "if I could kneel at her feet, if I could humble myself lower than the lowest negro to my dear mamma, and once hear her say she forgave me, I could be comforted; but I do not like to be comforted without this; I am angry at myself, and I ought to be angry."

"But, my dear little girl," replied Mrs. Harewood, "though you cannot thus humble yourself in your body, yet you are conscious that you are humbled in your mind, and that your penitence will render you guarded for the time to come; and let it be your consolation to know, though your mother is absent, the ears of your heavenly Father are ever open to your sorrows; and that, if you lament your sins to him, he will assuredly accept your repentance, and dispose the heart of your dear mother to accept it also. I sincerely pity you, not as heretofore, for your folly, but for your sorrow; and in order to enable you to comprehend what I mean by repenting before God, I will compose you a short prayer, which will both express your feelings, and remind you of your duty towards yourself and your mother."

Matilda received this act of kindness from her good friend with real gratitude; and when she had committed it to memory, and adopted it in addressing Almighty God, she found her spirits revive, with the hope that she should one day prove worthy of that kind parent, whom, when she lived with her, she was too apt to slight and disobey. As her judgment became more enlightened, she saw more clearly into the errors of her past education, and became perfectly aware that the love of her too-indulgent father had been productive of innumerable pains, as well as faults. She found herself much more happy now than she had ever been in her life; yet she had never so few indulgences—she had no slaves to wait on her, no little black children to execute her commands and submit to her temper; she was not coaxed to the dainties of a luxurious table, nor had costly clothes spread before her to court her choice, nor any foolish friend to repeat all she said, as if she were a prodigy of wit and talent; and all these things, she well remembered, were accorded to her as a kind of inheritance in Barbadoes; but, along with them, she remembered having violent passions, in which she committed excesses, for which she afterwards felt keen remorse, because she saw how they wounded her mother, and shamed even her doting father—ill-humour and low spirits, that rendered every thing irksome to her, and many pains and fevers, from which she was now entirely free; and she found, in the conversation, books, and instructions of her young friends, amusement to which nothing she had enjoyed before would bear comparison; for what in life is so delightful as knowledge, except the sense of having performed some particular benefit to our fellow-creatures?

CHAPTER VII

It will be readily supposed that, with the hopes now entertained of Matilda's conduct, Mrs. Harewood did not hesitate to provide the governess we have spoken of, and accordingly Miss Campbell was soon established in the family.

She found Matilda rapid in her ideas, persevering in her pursuits, but prone to resentment on every trifling occasion, and still subject to finding herself cause for repentance. On these occasions Miss Campbell conducted herself with composure and dignity, as if she considered a petulant child below the notice of a sensible woman: by this means the pride of the culprit was humbled; she was taught to retread her first steps, and perceive that she was an insignificant being, obliged to the suffrage of her friends, and only capable of being valuable in proportion to her docility and amiable conduct.

Mrs. Harewood had been accustomed to give her children the treat of a ball at Christmas; but on this year she put it off until midsummer, partly because she was afraid, in so large a party, and with such various dispositions, Matilda might not be able to conduct herself with perfect propriety during a whole evening, and partly because she wished her to learn to dance; for although this was, in her eyes, a very secondary accomplishment, when compared to solid knowledge, yet, as a healthful and innocent amusement, and called for in order to form the person in that station of life in which Matilda was likely to move, she desired to see her acquire at least as much of it as would preserve her from the appearance of awkwardness. It was an object of anxiety with this truly maternal friend to save her from all unnecessary mortification, at the same time she earnestly desired to see her tractable, humble, and gentle.

Time now passed away pleasantly, for all were occupied, and therefore happy: the idle are subject to many errors, and therefore many sorrows, from which the busy are exempt.

The good governess studied the temper and disposition of her pupils, and drew them forth in the happiest manner; not by making exhibitions of their attainments to others, but by showing them what was necessary to themselves for their improvement. She considered the work of education as sowing good seed, which shall spring up with vigour in advancing life, in proportion to the depth of the soil and its preparation for receiving it.

Whilst Miss Campbell inculcated those branches of polite learning which give a grace to virtue, she was still more desirous of inculcating virtue itself, by grafting it on religious principle, and that "fear of God, which is the beginning of wisdom."

The children of Mrs. Harewood had been taught, from their earliest days, that prudence and charity must go hand in hand; but it remained for Miss Campbell to impress this salutary truth on the mind of Matilda, who was naturally very generous, but debased that feeling by ostentation, and ever sought to indulge it with a vain and hurtful profusion, until she became enlightened by her young preceptress, who likewise, in many other points, regulated those desires in her pupils which blend good and evil, and require a firm and delicate management. She was very solicitous to render them active, both personally and mentally, knowing that the health of both body and mind depends upon their due exercise, and that a taste for study is yet perfectly compatible with those various exertions to which the duties of a woman always call her, in whatever sphere she may have occasion to move.

Miss Campbell wished to save her pupils alike from that perpetual fidgetiness, which renders so many females unable to amuse themselves for a single hour, unless their hands, feet, and tongue are employed, and that pertinacious love of reading, which renders them utterly unable to enter into the common claims of society, while a new story is perused, or a new study developed; she considered these errors as diseases in the mental habit it was her duty to prevent or eradicate, since they must be ever inconsistent with general duty and individual happiness.

Time passed—the vacation arrived, and the young people had the pleasure of all meeting again. Matilda was nearly as glad as Ellen to see Edmund and Charles, who, on their own parts, were much improved, and delighted to find the girls so. Matilda was in every respect altered, and although she had not Ellen's sweetness of temper, yet she had greatly conquered her propensity to passion, was very obliging in her general manners, and considerate to her inferiors, and attached to Ellen, her governess, and Mr. and Mrs. Harewood, with a tenderness and gratitude that was very amiable and even affecting.

CHAPTER VIII

One day, when Edmund and Charles had been at home about a week, the latter ran eagerly into the sitting-parlour, crying out—"Oh, mamma! there is Betty's sister down stairs, with the poor little twins in her arms, which were born just when Matilda came; they have short frocks now, but I perceive they have no shoes: suppose we young ones subscribe, and buy them some, poor things! there is my eighteen-penny piece for shoes, mamma—shoes, and hats too, if we can raise money enough."

Mrs. Harewood could not help smiling at Charles's eagerness, as she remembered the useful mortification he had experienced the last time his charity was called upon; and as she took up the money, she observed to him—"I am glad to see this, Charles; it is a proof you are more provident than you used to be; and, with your propensity to spending, it requires no little effort to save, in a large school, where there are always many temptations. I think your proposal is a very good one; and whilst I am collecting the money, pray step down stairs, and tell Betty to bring up the little innocents—we shall all be glad to see them."

Charles flew out of the room, and in less than a minute returned with the mother, carrying a babe in each arm. She was a very decent woman, the widow of a soldier, who died before his poor children were born; she now endeavoured to maintain herself and them by taking in washing, together with the pay of the parish, which, although small, she received very thankfully, and managed very carefully.

"Look, mamma! what pretty little feet they have," cried Ellen; "I am sure Charles was a good boy to think about shoes for them—was it not very kind of him, Matilda? because you know little boys seldom love little babies so much as girls do."

Matilda answered "yes," mechanically, for her mind was abstracted, and affected by the remembrance this scene was calculated to inspire. Mrs. Harewood, feeling for her evident embarrassment, sent the poor woman down stairs to take some refreshment, and then laid a three-shilling piece, as her own share of the contribution, besides Charles's subscription on the table.

Edmund laid a shilling on the table, saying—"If more is wanted, I will give you another with great pleasure: I hope, mamma, you *know* that I will?"

"Yes, Edmund, I *do* know that you will do any thing in your power, for you are regular and prudent, as well as a kind-hearted boy, and therefore have always got something to spare for the wants of others; I perceive, too, that you have the good sense to examine the nature of the claim made upon you, and that you give accordingly; *you* are aware, and I wish all the young ones to be so likewise, that this, although an act of charity, is not called for by any immediate distress; it is not one of those cases which wring the heart and drain the purse, for the poor woman is neither unprovided with lodgings nor food, and we ought always to keep something for the sake of sufferers of that description: I wish you, children, to be free and liberal, for we are told in the

Mrs. Hofland

scriptures that 'God loveth a cheerful giver;' but, in order to render you also frequent givers, you must be prudent ones."

"I have only one shilling in the world," said Ellen, laying it on the table.

"Then sixpence is as much as you ought to give," said Mrs. Harewood, giving her a sixpence in change, when, observing that she took it with an air of reluctance, she said—"My dear Ellen, be satisfied; you are a little girl, and have not half your brother's allowance, you know—it is sufficient."

While this was passing, Matilda had been fumbling in her pocket, and blushing excessively; her mind was full of painful recollections, yet fraught with gleams of satisfaction; but she wished very much to do two very contrary things, and whilst she still hesitated, Miss Campbell said—"Here is another sixpence, ma'am, which I will take, and give you an eighteen-pence, as I wish to give you a shilling, with Edmund's proviso."

"But," said Matilda, with a mixture of eagerness and hesitation, "then there will be no change for me, and I wish to give the same as Ellen; don't I want change, ma'am? I—I believe I do."

There was, in this confusion, and the blush which deepened in her cheek, a something which showed Mrs. Harewood a great deal of what was passing in the mind of this self-convicted, but compassionate and ingenuous girl. Mrs. Harewood took her shilling, and returned her sixpence, which she evidently received with pain, but an effort to smile, as Ellen had done, in return for the smile of her mamma.

After a short pause, Mrs. Harewood said—"Well, Matilda,

your delicacy is now satisfied—you have not affected any display of humanity, or ostentatious exhibition of wealth, in order to humble your young friends; but I perceive your heart is not satisfied; that heart is really interested in these babes, and, conscious that it is in your power to do more, you are mortified at stopping short of your own wishes and their wants."

"Oh dear, ma'am," replied Matilda, "you have read all the thoughts of my heart, (at least all but one,) and if you think it right, and Ellen will not think me proud, I will indeed be very glad if you will accept a crown for my subscription."

"I shall receive it with pleasure; and I can venture to assure you, that my children will neither feel envy, anger, nor any other emotion, except joy, at seeing the little objects of their care benefited, and you happy; for they have been taught only to value such actions, according to the motive in one party, and their usefulness to the other: but, Matilda, if it is not a very great secret, I should be glad to know what that *one* other thought in your heart was, which I did not guess, upon this occasion?"

Matilda did not find this question so easy of reply as Mrs. Harewood had expected it to be; she blushed and hung down her head; but, on perceiving that Mrs. Harewood was going to release her from all necessity of reply, she struggled to conquer what she deemed a weakness in herself, and answered thus—"Why, my dear madam, I was thinking what a little proud, stubborn, ill-behaved girl I was, at the time when these twins were born, and we first made a subscription for this poor woman; I remembered, too, how miserable I was, and altogether how much I had to lament, and I felt as if I could like to do something, to prove how thankful I am to God for bringing me into a family like yours, where every day of my life I may learn something good, and where I have been a great deal more happy than ever I was before, even in the house with my own parents."

Matilda stopped a moment, as if she thought her confession had perhaps infringed on her duty; but recollecting that all her past sorrow had been laid to the proper account, which was her own bad temper and pride, she again proceeded in it.

"When I thought on these things, I came close up to you; but my heart beat so quick, I could not speak, or else I had a guinea in my hand, the last my dear mamma gave me, and I wished very much to give you *that*; but then the memory of my foolish pride, the last time, came again into my mind—I became ashamed, and determined in all things to be guided by Ellen, who is almost a year older than I, and a great deal better."

"No, no—not *better*," said Ellen, warmly; and even her brothers, who loved her very dearly, struck with the same admiration of Matilda's frankness and generosity, exclaimed —"You are as good as Ellen *now*, Matilda—indeed you are!"

Mrs. Harewood, tenderly kissing her, assured her of her approbation, saying—"All you have said, my dear, tends decidedly to prove that your mind is indeed properly impressed with your duty both towards God and man, and that you have the most sincere desire to conquer those faults which you have already greatly amended; therefore I am determined to permit you to exercise your benevolence, in the most extensive manner that your heart could wish, knowing, as I do, that your fortune is fully equal to any act of charity, and that your good mamma will not fail to approve of it."

"Thank you, thank you, dear Mrs. Harewood! oh, you are my English mother, and I love you much more than any other person in the world, except my Barbadoes mamma."

The children eagerly crowded round their mother's chair, to hear what the good news was, which promised to benefit Sally, and make Matilda happy.

"I know," said Mrs. Harewood, "that the purchase of a mangle would set up the poor woman in her profession as a washerwoman, and enable her to earn at least ten shillings a-week more. It was my intention to purchase one for her myself at Christmas; but I could not do it before, as my charity-purse has been very much run upon lately. When Mr. Harewood comes in, I will ask for the money, and to-morrow we will all go in the coach, and see Matilda purchase it: but, my dear girl, suppose you just step and inform the poor woman of your intention, which I am certain you had rather do without witnesses; it will not only increase her pleasure, but enable her to prepare her apartment for such a noble and useful piece of furniture."

Matilda left the room, but returned almost immediately.

"You have been very quick," said Ellen, in rather a murmuring voice; "I wanted to know what she said and how she looked when you told her the good news."

"I did not speak to her myself—I commissioned Zebby to do it, for I knew it would give her quite as much pleasure as the poor woman herself could receive; and surely she has a right to receive every good I can bestow, as a slight atonement for the pain I have so very frequently given her."

Scarcely had Matilda given this proof of consideration and amiable feeling, when Sally and Zebby rushed into the room together, followed by Betty, who was truly grateful for the kindness thus bestowed on her sister.

Mrs. Hofland

Sally, with tears of joy, thanked her young benefactress; her words were few, but they were those of respect and thankfulness, and showed she was deeply sensible of the benefit she experienced.

Poor Zebby, delighted with the goodness of her young mistress, audibly expressed her pleasure, with all the characteristic warmth of her country, and not a little proud of those virtues which she fancied she had assisted to nurture.—"Oh," cried she, "dis be my own beautiful Missy own goodness; she makee joy in her mamma heart; she makee poor negro all happy—singee and dancee every body; no more whip, massa Buckraman—every body delight—every body glad—every body good Christian, when Missy go back!"

The spontaneous effusion of joy, uttered by this daughter of nature, affected all the party, and the joyful bustle had not subsided when Mr. Harewood entered. On being informed of the cause, he gave his full assent, and produced the money necessary for the purchase of the mangle.

The following day was pleasantly employed in arranging the poor woman's new acquisition; and when Matilda saw her grateful, happy countenance, and learned the manner in which the machine would be worked, and its usefulness in smoothing linen, she felt the value of a useful life, and a sense of her own importance, distinct from the idle consequence which is the result of vanity and pride, but perfectly compatible with the self-distrust and true humility which was now happily taking a deep root in her young mind.

Mrs. Harewood was gratified in perceiving such results of her maternal care for Matilda: still she did not relax in her vigilance; for she well knew, that along with corn will spring up tares in every young mind, and that the virtue of one day does not exempt from the vice of another, during the years of early life; and there were still many points in which the errors of her Barbadoes education were but too visible, and which called for the pruning hand of a sensible and pious friend.

CHAPTER IX

The foolish indulgence of Mr. Hanson had in no respect been more injurious to his only daughter, than in the unrestrained permission to eat whatever she liked, and as much of it as she could swallow.

On arriving at Mr. Harewood's, she found herself at a loss for many of the sweet and rich dishes she had been accustomed to eat of at her father's luxurious table; for although theirs was very well served, it consisted generally of plain and wholesome viands. Under these circumstances, Matilda made what she considered very poor dinners, and she endeavoured to supply her loss by procuring sweet things and trash, through the medium of Zebby, who, in this particular, was more liable to mislead her than any other person, because she knew to what she had been used, having frequently waited upon her, when the little gormandizer had eaten the whole of any delicacy which happened to be provided for the company.

Mrs. Harewood took great pains to correct this evil, especially on Ellen's account; for as Matilda was not covetous, she was ever ready to share with her only companion the raisins and almonds, figs, gingerbread, biscuits, or comfits, which she was continually munching; and this Mrs. Harewood had a particular objection to, not only because it is bad for the health, and lays the foundation for innumerable evils in the constitution, but because it renders young people hateful in their appearance, since nothing can be more unladylike or disagreeable, than the circumstance of being called to speak when the mouth is full, or displaying the greediness of their appetite, by cramming between meals, stealing out of a room to fill the mouth in the passage, or silently moving the jaws about, and being obliged to blush with shame when caught in such disgraceful tricks.

In order to guard against this habit, Mrs. Harewood positively forbade her servants from bringing any thing of the kind into the house; but poor Zebby, from habit, still obeyed her young Missy, and, besides, she had no idea that the enjoyments of fortune were good for any thing else than to pamper the appetite; so that it was a long time before she could be brought to desist from so pernicious a practice. As, however, the mind of Matilda strengthened, and she began to employ herself diligently in those new branches of education now imparted to her, she insensibly became weaned from this bad practice; and at length, inspired with a sincere desire to imitate her young friends, she broke herself entirely from this disgusting habit, and willingly adopted, in every thing, the simple wholesome fare partaken by her young friends.

It was undoubtedly owing to this temperance that she preserved her health, and even enjoyed it more than ever, notwithstanding the change of climate; but, alas! the good sense, resolution, and forbearance she thus acted with, was not followed by the humble companion of her voyage.

The change Zebby experienced in Mr. Harewood's comfortable kitchen, from the simple food to which, as a slave, she had been accustomed in the West Indies, was still greater, though in an exactly contrary line, than that of her young lady. Zebby soon learned to eat of the good roast and boiled

Mrs. Hofland

she sat down to, and exchanged the simple beverage of water for porter and beer, in consequence of which she became much disordered in her health; and when Mrs. Harewood prescribed a little necessary physic, as her mild persuasions were enforced by no threat, and the prescription appeared to the unenlightened negro a kind of punishment she had no inclination to endure, there was no getting her to swallow the bitter but salutary potion.

Zebby had been a long time feverish and subject to headaches, when the circumstance mentioned in the last chapter took place, which so exhilarated her spirits, that she declared she would be the first person who should use the new mangle which "her pretty Missy givee poor Sally."

It is well known that the negroes are naturally averse to bodily labour, and that, although their faithfulness and affection render them capable of enduring extreme hardship and many privations, yet they are rarely voluntarily industrious; and it was therefore a proof of Zebby's real kindness, that she thus exerted herself.

Unhappily, a mode of labour entirely new to her, and, in her present sickly state, requiring more strength than she possessed, although, had she used it freely some time before, it would have done her good, was now too much for her, and she came home complaining, in doleful accents, that "poor Zebby have achies all over—is sometimes so hot as Barbadoes, sometimes so cold as London."

Mrs. Harewood was well aware that the good-tempered negro was seized with fever, and she sent immediately for her apothecary, who confirmed her fears, and prescribed for her; but as there was no getting her to swallow medicine, he was obliged to bleed her, and put a blister on her head, which, however, did not prevent her from becoming delirious for several days.

Poor Zebby was, at this time, troubled with the most distressing desire to return to Barbadoes, and all her ravings were to this purpose; and they were naturally very affecting to Matilda, who never heard them without being a little desirous of uniting her own wishes to behold her native country, especially when she heard it coupled with the name of that only, and now fondly-beloved parent, from whom she was so far separated, and her tears flowed freely when she visited the bedside of the poor African. But her sorrow increased exceedingly when she learned the danger in which poor Zebby stood, and found that her death was daily expected by all around; bitter indeed were the tears she then shed, and she would have given the world to have recalled those hasty expressions, angry blows, and capricious actions, which had so often afflicted her humble attendant, whose fidelity, love, humility, and services, she now could fully estimate, and whose loss she would deeply deplore.

Mrs. Harewood endeavoured to comfort her under this affliction, by leading her to view the consolations which religion offers to the afflicted in general, and she explained the nature of that beneficent dispensation whereby the learned and the ignorant, the poor and the rich, the slave and his master, are alike brought to receive salvation as the free gift of God, through the mediation of our merciful Redeemer; and comforted her with the hope, that although poor Zebby's mind was but little enlightened, and her faith comparatively uninformed, yet as, to the best of her knowledge, she had been devout and humble, resting her claims for future happiness on that corner-stone, "the goodness of God in Christ Jesus," so there was no reason to fear that she would not leave this world for a far better, for "a house not made with hands, eternal in the heavens."

Matilda's mind was deeply impressed with this holy and happy consolation, but yet she could not help lamenting her own loss, in one whom she no longer considered her slave, and little better than a beast of burden, but as her countrywoman, her friend, the partaker of that precious faith by which alone the most wise, wealthy, and great, can hope to inherit the kingdom of heaven; and she could not help praying for her restoration to health, with all the fervour of which her heart was capable; and many a promise mingled with her prayer, that, if it pleased God to restore her, she would never treat her ill again: and these promises she likewise repeated to Mrs. Harewood and her governess.

Neither of these ladies lost the opportunity thus offered, of impressing on her mind the duties which every woman, whatever may be her rank or situation in life, does indeed owe to those whom Providence hath placed under her. They explained, in particular, the necessity of forbearance in point of manners, and of consideration in her daily employments— "If," said the good mistress, "I ring the bell twice or thrice, where once would answer every purpose, provided I gave myself the trouble of considering what I really wanted, I not only waste my servant's time, which would supply my wants, and therefore injure myself in one sense, but I waste the strength which is her only means of subsistence, and I awaken that vexation of temper, which, although perhaps suppressed before me, will yet rankle in her bosom, and probably induce her to commit some injury on my property, which is an actual sin in her: thus *my* folly leads to *her* guilt, and the very least mischief that can accrue is her unhappiness; for who can be happy whose temper is perpetually ruffled by the cruel thoughtlessness of those who have the absolute disposal of their time, their talents, and, in a great measure, their dispositions?"

"Depend upon it," added Miss Campbell, "that as we are

assured in the Scriptures, that 'for every idle word we shall be brought to account,' so, in a particular manner, must we be judged for all those idle words and actions which have inflicted on any of our fellow-creatures pains we have no right to bestow, or tempted them to sins they had no inclination to follow; the petty tyrannies of our whims, changes, and fancies—of our scoldings, complainings, peremptory orders, and causeless contradictions, will all one day swell that awful list of sins, of which it may be truly said, 'we cannot answer one in a thousand.'"

When Miss Campbell ceased speaking, Ellen, who, although not affected so violently as Matilda, had yet felt much for Zebby's situation, and was seriously desirous of profiting by all she heard, said in a low voice—"I will do every thing for myself—I will never trouble Susan, or Betty, or any body."

Mrs. Harewood knew the bent of her daughter's mind, and that although, from the sweetness of her temper and the mildness of her manners, she was not likely to fall into Matilda's errors, there were others of an opposite class, from which it was necessary to guard her; she therefore added— "Although consideration and kindness are certainly the first duties to be insisted upon in our conduct, yet there are others of not less importance. It is the place of every mistress to exact obedience to reasonable commands and the execution of all proper services. If she does not do this, she deserts her own station in society, defeats the intentions she was called to fulfil, and which made her the guide and guardian, not the companion and fellow-server, of her servants. In abandoning them to their own discretion, she lays upon them a burden which, either from ignorance or habit, they are probably unequal to endure, since it is certain that many truly respectable persons in this class have been only so while they were under the controlling eye or leading mind of their superiors. Besides, all uncommon levity of manners, like all unbecoming freedom in conversation, more frequently arises from weakness or idleness in the parties, and ought to be guarded against in our conduct, as never failing to be degradatory to ourselves, and very far from beneficial to those they affect to serve: it is possible to be very friendly, yet very firm; to be gentle, yet resolute, and at once a fellow-Christian and a good master to those whom Providence hath rendered our dependants."

Ellen listened to this with attention, and endeavoured to understand and apply it; but both she and Matilda continued to pay the most affectionate attentions to poor Zebby, whose disorder in a few days took a more favourable turn than could have been expected, although the delirium did not immediately subside, but rather affected her general temper, which, under its influence, appeared as remarkably unpleasant and tormenting to herself and all around, as it was formerly kind and obliging.

This period was indeed trying to Matilda, who was by no means sufficiently confirmed in her virtuous resolutions, or good habits, to endure reproaches where she merited thanks, even in a case where she was aware of deranged intellect and real affection, either of which ought to have led her to endure the wild sallies and troublesome pettishness of the suffering negro. It must however be allowed, that if she did not do all she ought, she yet did more than could have been once expected, and very greatly increased the esteem and approbation of her friends.

Matilda, when she was not influenced by the bodily indolence which was natural to her as a West-Indian, and which was rather a misfortune than her fault, was apt to be too active and bustling for the stillness required in a sick chamber; and whatever she did, was done with a rapidity and noisiness, more in unison with her own ardent desire of doing good, than the actual welfare of the person she sought to relieve; whereas Ellen never for a moment lost sight of that gentle care and considerate pity, which was natural to a mind attuned to tenderness from its very birth; and many a time would she say—"Hush, Matilda! don't speak so loud; have a care how you shut the door," &c.

One day they both happened to go in just as the nurse was going to give the patient a basin of broth—"Let me give it her," said Matilda; "you know she always likes me to give her any thing."

"Sometimes she does, when she knows you; but her head wanders to-day sadly."

"Never mind," replied Matilda, in her hurrying manner, and taking the broth from the woman in such a way that the basin shook upon the plate; on which Ellen said—"Have a care, the broth seems very hot; indeed, *too* hot for Zebby to take."

Matilda fancied this caution an indirect attack upon her care, and she went to the bedside immediately, and bolting up to the patient, who was sitting, raised by pillows, she offered the broth to her, saying—"Come, Zebby, let me feed you with this nice food—it will do you good."

The warm fume of the basin was offensive to the invalid— "Me no likee brothies," said she; and as it was not instantly removed, she unhappily pushed away the plate, and turned the scalding contents of the basin completely into the bosom of poor Matilda, as she reclined towards her.

Shrieking with pain, and stamping with anger, Matilda instantly cried out that she was murdered, and the wretch should be flayed alive.

Mrs. Hofland

Ellen, shocked, terrified, and truly sorry, called out in an agony—"Mamma, dear mamma, come here this moment! poor Matilda is scalded to death!"

The nurse, the servants, and Mrs. Harewood herself, were in a few moments with the sufferer; and the latter, although she despatched the footman for a surgeon, did not for a moment neglect the assistance and relief in her own power to bestow; she scraped some white lead[1] into a little thick cream, and applied it with a feather all over the scalded parts; and in a very short time the excruciating pain was relieved, and the fire so well drawn out by it, that when the surgeon arrived he made no change in the application, but desired it might be persisted in, and said—"He had no doubt of a cure being speedily obtained, if the patient were calm."

[1] The author has found this prescription very efficacious in various cases of scalds.

During the former part of this time, Matilda continued to scream incessantly, with the air of a person whose unmerited and intolerable sufferings gave a right to violence; and even when she became comparatively easy, she yet uttered bitter complaints against Zebby, as the cause of the mischief; never taking into consideration her own share of it, nor recollecting that she acted both thoughtlessly and stubbornly in neglecting the advice of Ellen; and that although her principal motive was the endeavour to benefit Zebby, yet there was a deficiency in actual kindness, when she offered her broth it was impossible for the poor creature to taste. Such, however, was the commiseration for her injury felt by all those around her, that no one would, in the moment of her punishment, say a word that could be deemed unkind; and soothings, rather than exhortations, were all that were uttered.

At length the storm was appeased; Matilda, declaring herself much easier, was laid upon the sofa, and a gentle anodyne being given to her, she closed her eyes, and if she did not sleep, she appeared in a state of stupor, which much resembled sleep. It so happened, that the hot liquid had, in falling, thrown many drops upon her face, which gave her so much pain at the moment, that she thought she was scalded much worse than she really was, as did those around her; but Ellen, as she watched her slumbers, now perceived that this was a very transient injury, and she observed to her mamma, that she hoped Matilda's good looks would not be spoiled by the accident, at least that her beauty would be restored before her mother's arrival from the West Indies.

"Before that time," returned Mrs. Harewood, "I trust Matilda will have attained such a degree of mental beauty, as would render the total destruction of her personal beauty a trifling loss, in comparison, to the eye of a thinking and good mother, such as I apprehend Mrs. Hanson to be."

"But surely, mamma, it is a good thing to be handsome? I mean, if people happen to be handsome, it is a pity they should lose their beauty."

"It is, my dear, to a certain degree a pity; for a pretty face, like a pleasant prospect, gives pleasure to the beholder, and leads the mind to contemplate the great Author of beauty in his works, and rejoice in the perfection every where visible in nature. The possessors of beauty may, however, so often spare it with advantage to themselves and their near connections, that the loss of it, provided there is neither sickness, nor any very disgusting appearance, left behind, does not appear to me a very great misfortune."

"But surely, mamma, people may be both very pretty and very good?"

"Undoubtedly, my dear; but such are the temptations handsome people are subject to, that they are much more frequently to be pitied than envied; yet envy from the illiberal and malicious seldom fails to pursue them; and when they are neither vain nor arrogant, generally points them out as both."

"I have often wished to be handsome, mamma, because I thought people would love me if I were; but if that is the case, I must have been mistaken, mamma."

"Indeed you were, my child; personal charms, however attractive to the eye, do not blind, or even engage the heart, unless they are accompanied by good qualities, which would have their effect, you know, without beauty—nay, even in ugly persons, when we become thoroughly acquainted with them. Can you suppose, Ellen, that if you were as handsome as the picture over the chimney-piece, that you would be more dear to me on that account, or that you would, in any respect, contribute more to my happiness?"

"You would not love me better, dear mamma, but yet you would be more proud of me, I should think."

"Then I must be a very weak woman to be proud of that which implied no merit, either in you or me, and which the merest accident might, as we perceive, destroy in a moment; but this I must add, that if, with extraordinary beauty, you possessed sufficient good sense to remain as simple in your manners, and as active in the pursuit of intellectual endowments, as I hope to see you, *then* I might be *proud* of you, as the usual expression is; for I beg you to remember that, strictly speaking, it is wrong to be proud of any thing."

"Zebby always said that Mr. Hanson was very proud of Matilda—I suppose it was of her beauty."

"I suppose so too, and you could not have brought forward a more decisive proof of the folly and sin of pride, and the inefficacy of beauty to procure love, than in the conduct and qualities of the persons in question. Mr. Hanson's pride of his daughter's beauty rendered him blind to her faults, or averse to correcting them; and from his indulgence, the effect of that very beauty for which he sacrificed every real excellence, was so completely impaired, that I am sure, with all your predilection for a pretty face, you will allow that Matilda, with all those red spots plastered with white ointment, is a thousand times more agreeable than Matilda with bright eyes and ruddy cheeks on her first landing."

"Oh yes, yes!" cried Ellen, looking at her with the tenderest affection, and relapsing into tears, which had frequently visited her eyes since the time of the terrible accident.

The opiate had now spent itself, and Matilda, giving a slight shudder, awoke, and looked at Ellen with a kind of recollective gaze, that recalled the events of the morning, and which was succeeded by a sense of pain.

"What is the matter, Ellen? you are crying—have you been scalded?"

"No," said the affectionate child, "but *you* have."

A confused recollection of all the particulars of the affair now came to Matilda's memory; and as by degrees they arose on her mind, she became ashamed of the extreme impatience she had exhibited, and surprised that Ellen could love and pity so much a girl whose conduct was so little likely to ensure affection and respect; and although the pain became every moment more troublesome, she forbore most magnanimously to complain, until the changes in her complexion induced Mrs. Harewood to say,—"I think,

Matilda, we had better apply the ointment again to your wound—you are still suffering from the fire, I see."

"If you please, ma'am."

With a light and skilful hand, Mrs. Harewood again touched the wounds, and immediate ease followed; but ere she had finished her tender operation, Matilda caught that kind hand, and, pressing it fondly to her lips, bathed it with her tears; they were those of gratitude and contrition.

"I fear you are in much pain *still*," said her kind friend, though she partly comprehended her feelings.

"Oh, no! you have given me ease; but if you had not, I would not have minded, I feared, indeed I am certain, that I behaved very ill, quite shamefully, this morning; and you are so—so good to me, that—that—"

Matilda was choked by her sobs, and Mrs. Harewood took the opportunity of soothing her, not by praising her for virtues she had not exercised, but by calling upon her to show them in her future conduct; although she did so far conciliate as to say, that the suddenness of the injury, in some measure, excused the violence she had manifested.

Matilda gave a deep sigh and shook her head, in a manner which manifested how far this went in palliation, and was aware that much of error remained unatoned. She inquired how Zebby was, and if she was sensible.

"She has been so ever since your accident, which appeared to recall her wandering senses by fixing them to one point; and as her fever is really abated, I trust she will soon be better."

Matilda hastily sprang from the sofa, and though in doing so she necessarily greatly increased the pain under which she laboured, yet she suppressed all complaint, and hurried forward to Zebby's room, followed by Mrs. Harewood and Ellen; the former of whom was extremely desirous at once to permit her to ease her heart, and yet to prevent her from injuring herself, by adding to the inflammation of her wound.

It was a truly affecting spectacle to behold Matilda soothing and comforting the poor black woman, who had not for a moment ceased to reproach herself, since the screams of the young lady had brought her to her senses, and her invectives to the knowledge of her own share in the transaction. It was in vain that the nurse and the servants of Mrs. Harewood had endeavoured to reconcile her, by the repeated assurance, that let the young lady say what she pleased, yet no harm could reach her: that in old England, every servant had law and justice as much on their side as their master could have.

This was no consolation to the faithful negro, who appeared rather to desire even unmerited punishment than seek for excuse; she incessantly upbraided herself for having killed pretty Missy, and breaking the heart of her good mistress; and when she beheld the plastered face of Matilda, these self-reproaches increased to the most distressing degree, and threatened a complete relapse to the disorder she had yet hardly escaped from.

"You could not help it, Zebby; it was all an accident, and ought to be chiefly attributed to my own foolishness," said Matilda.

"Oh, no! it was me bad and foolish. Missy, me naughty, *same* you used to be—pushee here and pushee there, in bad pets—it was all me—breaky heart of poor Missis—she comee over great seas; thinkee see you all good and pretty as Englis lady; and den you be shocking figure, all cover with spotee—oh deary! oh deary! perhaps come fever, then you go to the death, you will be bury in dark hole, and mamma never, *never* see you again."

The desponding tones of this speech went far beyond its words, and Matilda combining with it the caution she had heard the medical gentleman make respecting fever, and the first exclamation of Ellen, that—"Matilda was scalded to death," induced her to suppose that there was really danger in her case; and after repeatedly assuring Zebby of her entire forgiveness and regard, she returned to the apartment she had quitted, with a slow step, and an air of awe and solemnity, such as her friends had never witnessed before.

After Matilda had lain down on the sofa some minutes, she desired Ellen to get her materials for writing, but soon found that the pain in her breast rendered it impossible for her to execute her design.

"I will write for you," said Ellen.

"That won't do—I wanted, with my own hand, to assure dear mamma that poor Zebby was not to blame, nor any body else."

"My dear," said Mrs. Harewood, "we can do that by and by, when your mamma comes over."

"But if, ma'am—if I should *die?*"

Mrs. Harewood could scarcely forbear an inward smile, but she answered her with seriousness, and did not lose the opportunity of imprinting upon her mind many salutary truths connected with her present situation, not forgetting to impress strongly the necessity which every Christian has of being ever ready to obey that awful summons, which may be expected at any hour, and from which there is no appeal; but she concluded by an assurance that in a few days the present disorder would be completely removed, in case she guarded her own temper from impetuosity, and observed the regimen prescribed to her.

When Matilda's fears on this most important point were subsided, she adverted to her face, but it was only to inquire whether it was likely to be well before her mother came, she being naturally and properly desirous of saving her dear parent from any pain which could arise from her appearance; and when her fears on this head were likewise relieved, she became more composed in her spirits, and more anxious than ever to prove, by future good conduct, her sense of contrition for the past, and resolution for the future; and although she was most thankful for the sympathy of her friends, she never sought it by useless complainings, or aggravated her sufferings in order to win their pity or elicit their praise; and by her perseverance and patience, a cure was obtained much sooner than could have been expected from the nature of the accident.

Zebby regularly amended, as she perceived the great object of her anxiety amend also; and the sense she entertained of her late danger, the gratitude she felt for the kindness she had been treated with, and, above all, the self-denial to which she perceived her young lady accustomed herself, in order to recover, induced her henceforward to become temperate in her use of food, and tractable as to the means necessary for preserving her health, and to perceive her duty with regard to the commands given by her young lady, to whom she was now more truly attached than ever: for the attachment of improved minds goes far beyond that of ignorance.

CHAPTER X

When Matilda was fully recovered from the pain of her accident, her good friends had the satisfaction to perceive that the most salutary effects had arisen from the disposition with which she had borne it. She had become sensible how much we must all be indebted to our fellow-creatures, in any privation of health and ease, and this had taught her to be humble and thankful to all who contributed to her comfort; and from necessarily suppressing both her appetite and her temper, she had gained a command of both, which she had been a stranger to before. From being unable to join in any play requiring personal activity, she had been obliged to find her amusement in reading; and as that most excellent and delightful work, "The Parent's Assistant," by Miss Edgeworth, had been presented to her just before, she made herself completely mistress of those admirable tales, and by conversing much upon them with Mr. and Mrs. Harewood, with whom she usually sat, she became deeply imbued with all the important precepts they are intended to convey, as well as the stories they so agreeably relate.

One evening, when the whole family were assembled, the disorder which had afflicted Zebby became the subject of conversation; Miss Campbell observing, "that the poor woman had undoubtedly been as nervous as any fine lady, and therefore given another proof, in addition to the multitude which must affect every person of judgment and feeling, that there was indeed no difference of constitution, feeling, or character, between white people and black ones, when they were placed in similar circumstances."

"Certainly not," said Mr. Harewood, "and in a short time this doctrine will be more fully proved by the emancipation of all the blacks, who will, I trust, become diligent servants and happy householders, no longer the slaves of tyrants, but the servants of upright masters."

"But I am told, mamma," said Edmund, "that the proprietors of West India property will all be ruined; people say, this will come upon them as a retribution for past sins; but as many of these sins were committed in days that are past, and the present inhabitants, in many instances, have behaved exceedingly well, I must own I wish sincerely this may not be the case. Can you tell me any thing about it?"

"They all deserve to be ruined," interrupted Charles, "who have done such bad things as the planters do. Oh, how I wish I could be there when all the slaves are set at liberty! with what delight should I join in their universal shout of joy and freedom, and in all their innocent festivals!"

Edmund shook his head—"I should like the slaves to be happy as well as you; but I don't like for any body to be ruined, especially people who are so nerveless and inactive as those who have resided in warm islands; surely it is not true?"

Edmund looked again inquiringly.

"I am sorry to say," answered Mrs. Harewood, "that in many cases much suffering may be apprehended; but our government will undoubtedly soften every evil to the inhabitants, as far as they can do it consistent with their views: you know the emancipation of the slaves takes place gradually, and by that means enables people to collect their money, to divert the channels of their merchandise, or to make themselves friends of those who have hitherto been held by the arm of power only. The grand shout of a multitude restored to freedom is undoubtedly very attractive, and enough to warm the heart of a benevolent enthusiast like Charles; but it is not advisable to set food in great quantities before a starving man, lest he eat himself into a surfeit. Ignorance is always in danger of using power very ill, since we see that even the enlightened are frequently prone to misuse it."

"Then I hope, mamma, it will turn out better than people think; and there will be very little individual suffering from it."

"I am sorry to say, my dear, that notwithstanding what I have said, I yet fear many persons will suffer; I know a widow myself, who is returning to this country nearly destitute, after living many years in a state of luxury; very happily she has only one child, and has not suffered her past prosperity so to unnerve her mind, as to render her useless and desponding in the day of adversity. On the contrary, she has the magnanimity to rejoice in the freedom of the slaves, although that freedom has destroyed her fortune."

At this moment, every eye was involuntarily bent on Matilda, who, feeling undoubtedly some degree of compunction and shame, when she either thought on her own former conduct, or the state of her country, had kept aloof till now. At this moment she started, and, with a look of most anxious inquiry, she cried—"Oh, ma'am! surely you do not mean my poor mamma? And yet—yes, certainly you mean her—she has lived many years in prosperity—she has but one child, and she is possessed of a pious, good heart, and a kind, generous spirit, and would not wish the poor negroes to remain slaves—she would rather work herself than injure any body. Dear Miss Campbell, pray make me clever and good like yourself, and then I will be a governess, and get money, and support dear mamma—*indeed* I will."

The amazing rapidity with which these words were uttered, and the perturbation of spirits which accompanied them, prevented Matilda from perceiving that Mrs. Harewood was anxious to interrupt her; and even when that good friend began to speak, she was too much affected and disturbed to listen to her. She went on to say, with an agitated voice, but ingenuous countenance—"I cannot help crying, to be sure; but indeed I am not sorry that the poor slaves are to have their liberty, and I do not mind the money we have lost; I only want to see my dear mamma, and to comfort her, and to tell her that I would not be the mistress of bought slaves for all the world; for I *now* know that in the sight of God they are my equals, and if good, my superiors. I *know* that Jesus Christ died to save them as well as me, and that he will not forgive them who insult him, by daring to buy and sell those whom he has purchased with his own blood; and besides, I do not wish to possess them; for if I did, I should be proud and cruel and miserable, as I used to be."

The anxious, troubled heart of Matilda now found refuge in abundant tears, and, throwing herself on the bosom of her maternal friend, she shed them freely there; and as the storm of grief subsided, Mrs. Harewood obtained her attention to these words—"My dear Matilda, your vivid imagination, and the quickness of feeling, which even in a good cause is too apt to hurry you away, have led you into unnecessary trouble; it is not *your* mamma, but a Mrs. Weston, of Jamaica, of whom I spoke. I can, however, scarcely regret the pain you have experienced, because it has caused you to express sentiments which do you honour, and which must give great pleasure to your mother."

"But my mamma is coming over soon?"

"She *is*, my dear, but under very different circumstances, her property being all well disposed of, and settled in the English funds; and be it your comfort to know, that although your father was a proprietor of West India estates, yet his fortune was not accumulated by the infamous traffic to which we allude; although, like other people, he held slaves for the purposes of agriculture and domestic labour, he had an estate in this country, which enabled him to support an expensive establishment, without recurring to those practices too common among the planters in your country."

"And has the lady of whom you spoke no estate, no money, to support herself and her little girl?"

"She has *not*, my dear; but I trust her friends in England will provide her with some situation, in which her talents will enable her both to support herself and benefit others; and by this means the cup of affliction now may hereafter prove one of blessedness: her little girl is only six years old, and will therefore be but a trifling expense to her for some years to come."

Matilda now wiped her eyes, but was observed for a considerable time involved in deep thought, and silent thanksgiving to God, and no one around thought it right to interrupt the silent aspirations of her heart; but as soon as her countenance resumed its usual expression, and she rose from her seat, the young ones surrounded her, and with cheerful looks congratulated her on the change in her feelings, which they were aware a few moments must have produced; for, as Edmund observed, though it was very right to be resigned to every change which it pleased God to send, yet it was undoubtedly a great pleasure to know that a dear parent enjoyed not only the power of living in her usual style of comfort, but that she preserved the power of bestowing a part of her fortune to feed the poor, and to communicate knowledge, and sow the seeds of virtue in the minds of the young and uninformed.

Matilda listened to their congratulations with gratitude and pleasure, and looked forward with exultation, chastened by a proper diffidence of herself, to the time when, with her beloved mother, she should be employed in acts of beneficence and social enjoyment—"So passing through things temporal, as not to lose the things that are eternal."

CHAPTER XI

On the following midsummer vacation, Mrs. Harewood complied with the wishes of her young family, by consenting to give a ball to their young friends; and as she disapproved very much of late hours, the whole party were invited to dinner, in order that the dance might commence early.

The day previous to this entertainment was a very busy one, as the young people were permitted to display their taste by arranging the ball-room, and ornamenting it in the best manner they were able with flowers, under the inspection and with the assistance of Miss Campbell. The boys, attended by the footman, went out into the country, and returned laden with beautiful spoils from the hedges and copses, consisting of branches of trees, brushwood, and maythorn, together with those green plants which at this season of the year are found in abundance, such as clivers, coltswort, and the various mallows. When these were brought home, the young ladies tied gay flowers, made of various-coloured paper, upon them, at distances, with green worsted; and when these ornaments were finished, the branches themselves were tied together with strong cord, which was hidden by the foliage. By this means they were made into long wreaths, which were hung in festoons all round the room, and had an exceedingly beautiful effect, while over the doors and windows arches were formed of the same materials; but when the greens were brought nearer to the eye, natural flowers were used, which, being cut very short in the stem, preserved themselves fresh and beautiful, and perfumed the place with the most delightful odours.

Though this employment was charming, yet it was necessarily fatiguing, and the children went to bed at an early hour. Not long after they had retired, Mr. and Mrs. Harewood heard a carriage, and while they were conjecturing who it might be, to their great surprise, the long-expected stranger, Mrs. Hanson, was announced.

They were truly rejoiced to see her; for, although personally unknown to them, they were much disposed to esteem and love her, both from the style of her letters, and the many traits of her conduct and character given by Zebby, who was an able eulogist, since she ever spoke from the heart, and although ignorant, was by nature acute and penetrating.

The anxious mother, sensible that forms were not necessary to be attended to, in addressing the worthy couple to whom she came a welcome, though unknown guest, first inquired after her only child. When told that she was in bed, and fast asleep, having been much fatigued when she retired, she immediately declared that she would not have Matilda awoke for her own gratification—a declaration which confirmed the good opinion the family already entertained of her. She could not, however, resist the very natural desire she felt of beholding that dear object of her solicitude, from whom she had been so long parted; and she therefore visited her room, and, softly kissing her forehead, observed, to the great satisfaction of Mrs. Harewood, that she had never seen her look so well before, which was certainly the fact, though her weariness had induced some degree of paleness.

Tears rose to the eyes of the fond mother, and often, often

Mrs. Hofland

were they turned to the bed which contained all her earthly treasure, ere she could tear herself away; and Mrs. Harewood felt aware that silent prayers occupied her heart for the future welfare and progressive virtue of a being naturally so very dear, and whose bad passions, at the time of their parting, had given so little rational hope of future felicity, either to herself or her widowed parent. Sympathizing truly with her feelings, and aware of the extreme delicacy of the subject, especially to one of whose peculiar feelings she knew so little, Mrs. Harewood left it to time to show the change in Matilda.

Mrs. Hanson was recalled from the fond reverie the sight of her daughter had involved her in, by the voice of Zebby, who had only just learned the arrival of that dear mistress she had ever so justly estimated. The two ladies descended, and found the happy negro weeping for joy, and running about the breakfast-parlour and dining-room, seeking for her lady, whom, when she beheld, she danced about like a wild woman; one moment being ready to cast herself at her feet, and the next longing to embrace her.

"I am very glad to see you, Zebby," said Mrs. Hanson, "and very happy to find you still my daughter's servant, as I know you will suit her much better in many respects than any Englishwoman possibly could."

"Me love Missy ver much, madam, but me no Missy maid now; me housemaid for madam Harewood now; me makee de bed, sweepy de stair, do all sort ting; me never wait on Missy, no, never."

Mrs. Hanson gave a deep sigh, and said to Mrs. Harewood— "I fear you have had some trouble in procuring a maid for my daughter, ma'am?"

"When your daughter came to us, you may remember, my good madam, that we undertook to treat her in every respect as if she were our own; we *have* done it, and you will be able to judge to-morrow how far your dear girl is benefited or injured by sharing the attentions of Ellen's nursemaid, Ellen's governess, and Ellen's mother."

Mrs. Hanson felt that she was much indebted to the kindness evidently intended by this arrangement, especially as it was a plain case, that Zebby had been retained in the family for her accommodation; yet she could not help thinking that the contrast between Matilda's past and present situation was too great: although she had a thousand times desired that some great change might be adopted in her education, yet her heart shrunk at the idea of the discipline which she had so long felt to be necessary. She was afraid that the terrible passions her child had manifested, had rendered terrible changes necessary, and a train of inflictions and privations arose to her view, which maternal tenderness was unequal to contemplate unmoved; she therefore apologized to her friends, and retired to her room, but her pillow was strewed with those thorns which solicitude had planted there.

CHAPTER XII

The following morning the young people arose early, and were surprised to find Mrs. Harewood also stirring; her amiable, affectionate heart promised itself a treat, in witnessing the sweet emotions of Matilda, on hearing the joyful tidings of her mother's arrival; nor was she disappointed—the delighted girl manifested all the rapture of which her warm susceptible heart was capable; and on hearing her mother slept in the crimson room, was hastily bending her steps to the chamber, thus named from the colour of the bed.

"But, my dear, it is yet early; your mamma was much fatigued with her long journey from Falmouth: is it not a pity to disturb her, especially as she has already seen and kissed you, although she would not awake you?"

Matilda stopped—"I do *so* wish to see mamma," said she, "and to hear her speak! but then to awake her for my own pleasure would be selfish, as I used to be—I won't be selfish."

"That's right, my dear—you are now proving yourself truly affectionate—you are preferring mamma to yourself."

"But I may just stand at the door and listen to her breathing, and so wait till she moves."

"Certainly, my dear."

Away flew Matilda, happiest of the happy; and she had scarcely been ten minutes on her station when Mrs. Hanson's bell rang, and Matilda instantly opened the door, in silent but delightful expectation.

"Is my daughter awake?" said the fond mother.

"Oh, yes, yes, dear mamma, I am here!" cried she, springing to the outstretched arms of her loved parent, who, in embracing her joyfully, yet felt solicitude mingle with her joy, from the consciousness that her earthly happiness was centred in this single object, and that upon her future conduct rested the peace of both.

Mrs. Hanson did not rise for some hours, and her daughter breakfasted with her, and spent the time principally in making inquiries after their old friends in Barbadoes, so that Mrs. Hanson had no opportunity of observing how her daughter was looked upon in the family, and on this eventful day, the ball in the evening was naturally the subject uppermost on Matilda's mind, so that there was yet no development of her real improvement.

At length Mrs. Hanson arose; her maid came in to dress her, and whilst this took place, the mother beheld with delight the improvement which had taken place in her darling's person, which was taller, and considerably better formed, as she had cured herself of stooping, and all her motions indicated sprightliness and agility.

Whilst Mrs. Hanson congratulated herself on this appearance, Zebby tapped at the door, and, on being admitted, said, with a very long face and doleful accent—"Oh dear, Missy, very bad ting have happened; de milliner have sentee

Mrs. Hofland

home Miss Ellen new frock, and no sentee yours. She say she cannot makee till next week, because she very busy for little girls that losee their mamma, and must have blackee clothes to-morrow day."

Mrs. Hanson's heart sunk, and she felt as if her pleasure for this day at least was over, for she fully expected to see Matilda fly into a rage with the messenger, the milliner, and indeed all the house; and she could scarcely believe her own senses, when Matilda replied calmly—"Well, Zebby, it cannot be helped, and it does not signify much; I am sure Mrs. Harewood will excuse my want of a new dress on this occasion. To be sure, I should have liked to look the same as dear Ellen; but how can I think of such a trifling disappointment, when I remember it was caused by those unhappy children, who are now mourning for their mamma?"

So saying, she turned, and eagerly threw her arms round a mother, who, in the course of her whole life, had not embraced her with equal satisfaction; but before she had time to express her pleasure, and injure her who caused it, by the exaggerated praise which sprung to her lips, Matilda had run down stairs, just to peep at Ellen's new dress, speak of the delight she experienced in having gained her mother's society, and consult Miss Campbell as to the frock she must substitute for the one intended to be worn; and when Mrs. Hanson was left alone, she almost fancied that the foregoing scene was a kind of drama, which had been introduced for the purpose of surprising and pleasing her.

But observation confirmed her hopes, and justified her happiness. She descended at dinner-time, and was introduced to the children of the family, who, although little seen among so large a party, yet won her regard, from the unaffected kindness and ease with which they treated her daughter; and she observed, with approbation, that Matilda and Ellen were dressed exactly alike; the latter having declined wearing the frock bought for her, since her friend's could not be procured. Mrs. Hanson could not fail to love Ellen, in whose countenance the good temper, modesty, and sensibility which characterized her, were strongly expressed; but she had not much time to comment upon it, for the young party were now coming in, and attention was in some degree divided. In a short time dinner was announced, and the company, about thirty in number, were soon commodiously arranged round the hospitable table.

Mrs. Harewood had thought it right to disperse her own family among her guests, in order that they might pay proper attention to those near them, as by that means she hoped that none of the invited would be neglected; and according to this arrangement, which was made the preceding day, Matilda took the place appointed for her, which happened to be at some distance from her mamma, who sat, of course, next to Mrs. Harewood. In the bustle of so large a party, Mrs. Hanson could scarcely observe even her daughter at the beginning of the meal; but when the second course came in, she saw with some pain a large dish of custards placed exactly before Matilda; and on one of the company observing she had never seen such a noble dish of custards before, Mrs. Hanson said—"Matilda is remarkably fond of them; I am sorry they are so near her, for they are not wholesome."

"We seldom have such things on that account," said Mrs. Harewood; "but I must own I think them well placed, because Matilda can help her friends to them with ease."

These words drew the attention of the young ones, and Matilda soon received so many plates to supply, that there appeared little probability of her sharing in the feast. Edmund was near her, and gladly receiving his mother's approving smile, he secured one for Matilda, which he put upon her plate just before the last was demanded.

Ellen was equally busy distributing tarts near the bottom of the table. The footman brought her a custard, which he said Miss Hanson had sent for her.

"She is very good," said Ellen, "but I had rather take a jelly, if she will excuse my returning it."

The happy mother perceived that Matilda had sent Ellen the very custard which Edmund's kindness had ensured for *her*. Delicious tears sprang to her eyes; she perceived that Matilda was indeed a different creature; that she had not only conquered a disgraceful propensity, but acquired a habit of generous attention to others, of which there was at one period no hopes in her character.

The dancing now commenced, and the West Indian acquitted herself with great propriety; for although she did not perform so well as the greater part of the company, yet she was never awkward; and when at a loss for the figure, she listened with modesty, and obeyed with precision the rules laid down to her. Many of the party now assembled were amiable and obliging, but in so large a number, some were of course present, whose manners were less agreeable: but as Matilda considered herself one of the family, so she deemed it her duty to partake their cares, and render every person as happy as possible. She neither suffered rudeness to disturb her temper, nor awkwardness to excite her contempt; her conduct, under every temptation of this nature, was uniformly marked by self-command, modesty, and civility.

There was in this young party two Master Eustons, who, happening to be richer and a little older than the rest of the party, thought themselves entitled to quiz all around them at some times, and lord it over them at others. On their first coming into the room, they sought out Matilda, as a proper companion for them, because they had heard her named as a great West-Indian heiress; but when they saw her a modest, unassuming girl, they rather shunned her, as not being likely to enter into their sports. These boys would not have been voluntarily chosen as companions for his own by such a careful and observant father as Mr. Harewood, but they were the nephews of an old friend of his, and were then on a visit to their uncle, who would have felt himself neglected if Mr. Harewood had not invited them; and as, that gentleman very justly observed to his excellent lady, his children must necessarily mix with the world, both at school and elsewhere, it was desirable that they should do it sometimes under the eye of those kind parents, who might teach them how to distinguish what was good, and lead them, from general company, to choose particular society.

There was also a young lady who wished to render herself the particular companion of Matilda, for the same reason the Eustons had done, because she considered her the most wealthy child in the place; and from her person, and the elegance she observed in her mamma's dress and manners, she concluded that in a few years she would be the most dashing. It is astonishing how soon the eye of even a child can discriminate, in that particular which has been rendered the sole subject of its studies and the grand object of its wishes; so that people who pique themselves upon being men of the world, or women of fashion, are rivalled in all their boasted knowledge and discernment by young creatures, whose faculties they may deem very inefficient, and which are indeed so in all the higher requisites of mind and the attainments of knowledge.

The parents of Miss Holdup, the young lady in question, had acquired a large fortune, but were both called, at a very early period, from the enjoyment of it; and this their only child was placed, by the will of her father, under the sole guardianship of his solicitor, a man of integrity and of large fortune, and without any children of his own; so that the little girl had apparently every blessing her desolate situation demanded, for kindness was accorded to her in the family, as an orphan, without a rival, and her fortune was well secured by the skill of her guardian.

But, alas! false judgment and mistaken indulgence rendered this situation totally subversive of her improvement and her happiness; the lady to whose care she was immediately consigned was a vain and dissipated woman, who had no greater pleasure than in spending the fortune, laboriously acquired by her industrious spouse, in all the various amusements the metropolis presents to the idle and extravagant part of the community; and although she was what is generally termed a very good-natured woman, yet the moment her schemes of diversion or expense were thwarted, she could be as pettish, sullen, or even vulgar and violent, as the lowest servant. She piqued herself on being a woman of family, and when little Miss Holdup came into her household, the first care she took with her was to eradicate, as far as possible, the memory of her parents, and all their former connections, from her mind.—"My dear child, now you are, by great good fortune, got into a gentleman's family, remember you must never mention those creatures in the city your mamma used to visit. I must have no cheese-factor cousins introduced at my table; no, nor even the great linen-draper's daughter that gave you the doll; you have money enough to buy dolls of your own, and must have no more concern with those kind of people now."

"But," said the child, "I suppose I may talk about Miss Turner and her sister Anne, because they nursed me through the measles, and my father said I must always be grateful—I suppose he meant thankful, ma'am, for their kindness."

"Who are they, child? if they are decent people, it alters the case entirely."

"They are not decent people," said the child, pettishly; "they are very genteel people, and dress quite beautifully, and have a country-house, where I have played many a time; and they have a fine instrument, and more books than you have, and I love them dearly."

"But who are they, my dear?"

"Why, to be sure, they are their father's daughters, Mr. Turner, the great baker; every body knows Mr. Turner's shop, I suppose."

The lady was distressed. She began a speech, endeavouring to prove, that although gratitude was very good in its place, yet, when it was advisable to forget its object, then it was no longer good, but foolish, and improper, and unfashionable; but she checked herself in the midst of this exordium, by recollecting that the intellects of her pupil were unequal to all investigation, but that her inclination, youth, and temper could be more easily wrought upon. She began to load her with finery, take her to the play, though she fell asleep in the second act, speak of her in her own hearing as a wit and a beauty, shake her head knowingly whenever her city connections were alluded to; and therefore it was no wonder that in a short time the child forgot the friends she had loved, grew ashamed of the parents she had honoured, learnt to prattle on subjects of which she knew nothing, and to affect all the premature airs of a woman, with more than the usual ignorance of a child, as children are now usually instructed.

Perhaps a womanized child of this description is the most

Mrs. Hofland

disagreeable thing in existence, and is rendered only the more so, from any talent or natural acuteness it may happen to possess, since that never fails to give a spice of sin to what would otherwise be mere folly. The thinking mind shudders at the airs of infantine coquetry and malicious sneers, which are merely ludicrous to another stander-by; but how any person can be either indifferent to such a waste and perversion of human nature, or behold it with pleasure, is inconceivable. Mrs. Thornton was, however, so far the dupe of her own folly, that she conceived Miss Holdup the finest child she had ever known, and a decisive proof of her own talents for education. It was true, she had lavished upon her all her stores of information, in the same way that, agreeably to her own notions of dress and pleasure, she had expended upon her sums which her husband thought prodigious; and the result of both had been to make her what might be truly called a grand serious pantomime, or an artificial curiosity, for nature was completely banished her composition.

"Look at my lovely ward," she would exclaim, in rapture; "how totally different she is from any other child! she will never be mistaken for one of the lower order!"

True; but neither could she be mistaken for a gentlewoman: the appearance of the child was that of a figurante, ready equipped for her part at the opera; for, although in her twelfth year, she wore trowsers and petticoats that did not reach to her knees; they were, it is true, trimmed with the most costly Mechlin, formed by the most tasteful milliner; but as her shape was by no means graceful, and her mode of life, by harassing her into puny ill health, kept her wretchedly thin, she resembled at a distance a small windmill about to be set in motion; and when near her, it was impossible not to believe that her clothes had been stripped to the middle, for the sake of washing her bony shoulders perfectly clean.

But, alas! the interior was more naked, or dressed in some parts merely for exhibition: the poor child knew the steps of the last new dance and the name of new music; she could finger a little, and knew a few words of French from the vocabulary; but to the history of her country she was a perfect stranger, and, what was far worse, was ignorant of all religion, all duties. When she was out of temper, which was an increasing evil as she grew up, she was told only that it "spoiled her face;" if she were guilty of gluttony, she was warned against injuring her shape; but the real motive of good action, the foundation of pure principles, the necessity of self-control, were utterly unknown to her; she never saw them acted upon, nor heard them explained.

Such was the girl who now, with a bustling parade of affection, singled out Matilda as the only child whom she thought worthy of her patronage, and whom she intended to win and to use, when it suited her, in the very same way that ladies of twice her age so frequently make their selection of friends in the acquaintance of an hour.

Miss Holdup was disappointed in perceiving that Matilda did not act as if she were much pleased, or much flattered, by her partiality; but this she imputed to pride, and being very proud herself, she concluded that, on a little farther acquaintance, it would only render them better friends. Besides, she observed that Ellen was at present the dearest friend of Matilda; and although she considered this a degrading choice, yet she had patience to wait, and cunning enough to aid, the time when Matilda should see the superiority of such a girl as herself to poor Ellen, whom she concluded to be simple, because she perceived her to be modest and mild.

In the blithesome round of gaiety inspired by dancing, designs and airs of all kinds were for a time forgotten, and the sprightly movements of the feet kept pace with the hilarity of heart which banishes, for a time, all those unnatural combinations which disgrace the ingenuous breast of early life; but when a pause was given for the purpose of refreshment, various little parties were formed for conversation, and Miss Holdup contrived to monopolize Matilda, in a way that was painful to Ellen, disrespectful to the rest of the party, and embarrassing to her who was thus singled out; who became, with some, an object of envy, because the most fashionable girl distinguished her; with others, one of contempt, for the same reason. It will be readily conceived that Miss Holdup was never insignificant: where she did not attract admiration, she never failed to excite contempt: and as the party were, of course, for the most part amiable and well-educated children, whom Mr. and Mrs. Harewood held up as examples to their own, so the greater number, by many, regarded this young lady as a weak, ridiculous girl, whose appearance excited surprise and disgust, and whom nothing but good manners could prevent them from laughing at; and Matilda felt herself involved, from her union with her, in that kind of snare which, of all others, was the most galling to her, as from her very cradle she could never endure to be laughed at.

Mrs. Harewood perceived, from the expression of her countenance, that she laboured under very considerable vexation, and she was at times afraid that, by some irritating expression or haughty toss, Matilda would tarnish the honours of the day, by giving a pang to the heart of that fond and still happy parent, whose eyes were continually bent upon her, but who wished to see her act on the present occasion, without those influences her more immediate presence was likely to inspire. While with all the anxiety of a true friend, this good lady watched Matilda, a quick rattling sound was heard against the windows, and Matilda, a little surprised by the sound, and desirous of escaping the tedious and affected conversation of Miss Holdup, inquired what it was that she heard.

"Quiz the West Indian," said the younger Euston; "she never saw it hail before."

With a very grave face, the elder immediately came up to her, and told her it was raining comfits—"If you please," said he, "you may see them through the windows, for it is not dark, though the moon is clouded."

Matilda went eagerly to the window, for she was curious to observe a phenomenon entirely new to her. She soon perceived thousands of little balls, that fell as hard as stones, lying on the ground and the window frames, and she was desirous of examining them further; but just as she was turning to make inquiries of her friend Edmund, young Euston interrupted her, by saying—"Well, Miss Hanson, you now see the comfits; would you like to taste them? if you please, I will get you a spoonful."

"I should like to have a few certainly," replied she, "and will feel obliged to you to procure me some of them."

"Hush, hush!" said the young ones to each other, all desirous to see how Matilda would look, many merely from that love of play which is inherent at their age, others from a malicious spirit which is too frequently blended with a passion for fun. Mr. Harewood apparently took no notice, but he hovered about them, and had the satisfaction of hearing several girls condemn the Eustons, and profess an intention of saving Matilda from swallowing the cold hailstones.

"You may be easy," said Edmund, as they stood consulting together on the subject, when in ran the youth with eagerness, crying—"Here is a spoonful of beautiful comfits; now

Mrs. Hofland

open your mouth and shut your eyes—that is the way to taste them in perfection."

"Thank you, sir; I do not want to eat them; I know they must be snow, some kind of condensed snow, or ice, and I wished to examine them."

"Snow! how you talk!—it never snows in July."

"It never snows at all in my country—of course I know little about it; but unless Edmund assures me to the contrary, I shall certainly conclude that these little balls are frozen raindrops, of the same nature with snow."

"You are perfectly right, Matilda," said Edmund, "and you have quizzed your quizzers very completely."

"Miss Hanson has studied natural philosophy," said a young lady, sneeringly, being one of those who sought Miss Holdup's acquaintance. "I always thought that young ladies in the West India islands studied physical subjects more than any other."

"Physical subjects!" exclaimed several of the party; "how very strange a study! what a very singular thing for girls to think of!"

"I think you are quite mistaken," said Ellen, with more spirit than was usual to her; for, although she could not conceive that there was any harm in the study, she saw plainly that some spleen was intended against Matilda, and she loved her too dearly, to stand by whilst any wound was inflicted which her interference might avert. Though the most gentle and unoffending in her nature, yet she was capable of warm and active friendship, and, of course, was not a little astounded and hurt when the young lady replied—"Surely, Miss

Harewood, you cannot be ignorant that all our great medical practitioners torture and kill animals, for the purpose of ascertaining the nature of diseases, and, in many cases, undoubtedly for the purpose of learning how much suffering bodies of a certain size and texture are capable of enduring? Now I don't doubt, Miss Hanson, being so wise in other matters, can tell you exactly how much pain is necessary to kill a slave, how many stripes a child can endure, and how long hunger, beating, and torturing, may be applied without producing death; and prove that in case they do destroy a few blackies, that don't signify, if they can afford to buy more."

"Well, and suppose Miss Hanson did kill some of those creatures," cried Miss Holdup, "she can afford to buy more; at least, her mamma can, which is much the same; though to be sure, 'tis a fine thing to be independent. For my part, I think there is ten times more said about those filthy negroes than signifies: dear me! they are not to compare to my Frisky; 'tis the most angelic creature of a dog! worth fifty blacks any day, unless, to be sure, they were in handsome liveries."

Matilda had suffered in every nerve while the first lady spoke, but the defence of the second hurt her ten times more, as it appeared to indicate a hardness of heart, a daring to make light of a most solemn subject, and one to which she had given much serious thought, and she hastily plucked away the arm Miss Holdup had taken, and would have retired, but she was hemmed in by a circle, and could not escape. The young lady replied to her advocate, in a fawning voice—"Ah, dear Miss Holdup! you are fond of defending any body you take a fancy for; but I am certain, if you were really on the spot, you could not bear to *see* those things your *new* friend has been in the habit of *doing*. I am told, mere children amuse themselves in Barbadoes with sticking pins into the legs of little children, dropping scalding sealing-wax upon their arms, and cutting lines and stars in their necks with knives and scissors."

"Yes," added one of the Eustons, "and the most delicate ladies are waited upon by naked slaves, whose bare backs are probably bleeding from the recent effects of a sound whipping, inflicted, probably, because Missy's dolly had fallen, and broken her nose, out of Missy's own hands."

"Shocking creatures!"—"Dreadful wretches!"—"Wicked creatures!"—"How terrible!"—"How abominable!" were exclamations naturally uttered on every side, and those who, on Matilda's innocent triumph, had in the first instance pressed around her, now withdrew from her side, shrinking as from something monstrous and loathsome in nature; and such was the bustle and confusion between those who were eager to inquire, and those who were more eager to inform, that the few who endeavoured to divert attention from the subject, or insist upon the pictures presented being overcharged, could not be heard.

Matilda, overwhelmed with burning blushes, was utterly unable to articulate a syllable, much less to stem the torrent which, in accusing her country in general terms, was aimed at her in particular: her conscience accused her of many crimes, which, though far removed from atrocity like this, were yet utterly unjustifiable, and, as she now believed, might have led to the utmost limits of tyranny, cruelty, and oppression; and all she felt or feared in her own conduct, seemed to rise to her memory, and stamp conscious guilt on her expressive features; and while thus labouring under the torments of a wounded spirit, the Eustons, rejoicing in her confusion, pointed it out as a certain proof of her conscience upbraiding her, and a fresh volley of crimes and accusations were poured forth. It was in vain that Edmund attempted to be heard, and that Charles challenged every one to fight in her behalf, and that Ellen, with distressed vociferation and tears gushing into her eyes, kept again and again exclaiming —"It is *not* true—I am sure it is not; there are many good people in the West Indies, and nobody can be so wicked in the wide world. You tell these tales on purpose to make us ill—fie! fie!"

The agonized countenance of Ellen, by presenting a striking contrast to its usual expression of mild benevolence, told Mr. Harewood it was time for him to interfere. He had, for some minutes, hovered near, perceiving some kind of conspiracy, and thinking that his presence would be less observed than that of either of the ladies; and at his near approach, the aggrieved, accused, discomfited Matilda, whose eyes had been long cast on the ground, ventured to look up; for although she had a considerable general feeling of awe for Mr. Harewood, yet she had the most perfect reliance on his justice and kindness; and ashamed and conscious of past error as she now was, she yet felt assured of his protection and mercy.

The moment her eye met his, she felt all her hopes confirmed; and in the joy and exultation it gave her, she acquired strength to burst through the crowd; rushing forward, she sought refuge in his arms, and laid her burning cheek on the kind hand he extended towards her.

Ellen, at this moment, was, for the first time, attended to, as she cried out, with still stronger pathos—"Dear papa, I am so glad you are here! for you will tell us the *truth*—you will convince every body, that people in the West Indies do not torture their poor slaves for nothing but their own wicked pleasure."

"My dear little advocate, as I have never been in the West Indies, I have no right to contradict such evidence as has

Mrs. Hofland

been brought forward by respectable witnesses."

A cry of exultation began to pass the lips of the Euston party; but they were silent, as Mr. Harewood began to speak again.

"I am the more inclined to think these cruelties may sometimes take place in our islands, because I have myself witnessed similar effects in this country, where the barbarians who practised them were much curtailed in their power, and proved rather the disposition than the actual treatment of which you speak towards their unhappy victims."

"Indeed!" exclaimed they, with anxious curiosity, pressing nearer to the speaker.

"Yes," added Mr. Harewood, raising his voice, and assuming a serious aspect, "I have this very evening heard words applied to the heart of an unoffending individual, more painful than the lash, and seen looks directed against her, more torturing than any of the hateful operations you have mentioned; and I have not the least hesitation in saying, that those who could thus treat an amiable fellow-creature, and one who, as a stranger, is thrown upon their kindness, and entitled at least to their politeness, would, if they had the power, wound the body also, and might, by hardening their hearts against the claims of humanity, in a short time become capable of every possible enormity."

An awful silence, strikingly contrasted with the late lively dance and its following conversational bustle, now sat on every tongue; the self-convicted were ashamed of their conduct, the doubtful satisfied, and the friendly delighted; and desirous of stamping an important lesson, in the moment of awakened feeling and intelligence, Mr. Harewood continued to say—"Human nature, alas! is full of bad propensities; and when situation and the power of indulgence strengthen them, no wonder that man becomes selfish first, then hard-hearted, and lastly, even ferocious towards others. When, enlightened by education and taught by religion, he rises from this state of barbarity, and becomes not only civilized, but humane, gentle, condescending, and charitable, he merits great praise, for he has achieved great labour—he has conquered great difficulty; the very angels in heaven rejoice over him; and this child, this blushing, trembling, self-condemning, but self-corrected child, has done this. Look up, my dear Matilda! let who will sneer at you, I am proud of you; and there is not one person present who would not honour themselves, if they could secure your friendship. I was the first to correct you, nor will I ever flatter you; but I will always protect and defend you, so long as you continue to merit the high regard I now feel for you."

The sweetest tears she had ever shed now ran down the cheeks of Matilda, as Mr. Harewood pronounced this eulogy; and it will be easily conceived, that all the really good and sensible part of the company eagerly sought to soothe her spirits, and convince her of their regard, while her late tormentors either slunk away, as much ashamed as they were despised, or by an ingenuous confession of error, paved the way for returning esteem.

Miss Holdup arrogated to herself great praise for having defended what she called the right side; and so delighted was poor Ellen with every body and every thing which favoured her young friend, that she began to take a great fancy to the silly affected girl, merely because she thought that she loved Matilda; but Matilda herself felt that her severest pang had arisen from the very defence thus adopted; and while she thanked Miss Holdup for her good wishes, she yet shrank more than ever from forming an intimate acquaintance with one whom she considered as little better than an automaton figure on which fine clothes might be hung, and whose tongue had been taught to move, for the purpose of repeating the silly gibberish which ill-formed women repeat to uninformed children, in order to render them as stupid, proud, and silly as themselves.

On the following day, the party were naturally the subject of conversation, and Mrs. Hanson had great pleasure in finding that the bedizened doll, who had been so decidedly her daughter's companion the evening before, was by no means her chosen one, that distinction being reserved for Ellen only, whose kind heart would have been almost broken, had she imagined such a partiality indeed reciprocal, but who was as free from jealousy of Miss Holdup, as she was full of confidence in Matilda.

Mrs. Harewood on this occasion remarked, that she had never seen two girls more likely to form a mutual and lasting friendship than Ellen and Matilda, because they were likely mutually to benefit each other, since they would, she trusted, possess the same good principles and dispositions, but each having a character of her own, would become serviceable to the other. Matilda had more discrimination and firmness than Ellen, who, on her part, had a forbearance, patience, and gentleness, which nature as well as habit had in a degree left her friend but poorly provided with; but she said it would not be surprising if their mutual affection and reciprocal admiration should, in time, ingraft the virtues of each upon the other, and she hoped to see Matilda as meek as Ellen, and Ellen as firm and energetic as Matilda.

CHAPTER XIII

The happy family-party at Mr. Harewood's was necessarily soon broken up, as Mrs. Hanson took a house at Brompton, on account of the mildness of the air, and the young friends were then separated. Their removal was facilitated by the arrival of that West-Indian lady and her little girl, whom we have already mentioned, as being stripped of nearly all her possessions, and whom Mr. and Mrs. Harewood were desirous of accommodating in their house, until some plan for her future situation should be fixed upon. They were not of that number who can receive a rich friend with pleasure, and leave a poor one to shift for themselves; on the contrary, Mrs. Weston and her little Harriet were received by them, not only with affection, but with all consideration due to her former situation.

As soon as Mrs. Hanson had arranged her household at Brompton, she hastened to invite Mr. and Mrs. Harewood and their family to spend an early day with her, and was then introduced to Mrs. Weston, whom she knew well by report, and for whose altered situation she was truly concerned, especially after she became acquainted with her, as the suavity of her manners, the quiet dignity of mind, and unaffected resignation with which she bore her misfortunes, could not fail to prepossess her in favour of so wise and good a sufferer, who was likewise so cheerful and willing to be happy.

Harriet was a little girl, about six years old at this time, a tolerably good child but certainly subject to the same errors (though in a far less degree) which had formerly distinguished Matilda; and as she wanted incessantly somebody to do something for her, and there was no longer a slave at her command, her mother was too frequently obliged to be that servant—a circumstance which rendered the young Harewoods much less fond of Harriet than they would otherwise have been, and which, at times, tried the temper of even the gentle Ellen.

Matilda's whole mind was absorbed by this little girl, on whom she continually cast looks of the deepest interest; her mother imputed the serious air she wore to a regret very natural at her age, on revisiting the house where she had been so happy, and she felt some fears lest it should continue to haunt her mind: she had likewise many forebodings as to the future education of her daughter, being sensible that she had enjoyed advantages in Mr. Harewood's house of no common character; and she very candidly related all that was passing in her mind to that kind lady, whose maternal love for her child rendered her the most proper judge for the future, as she had proved herself the truest friend for the past.

Mrs. Harewood very strenuously recommended her to procure a good governess for her daughter, as it was hardly to be expected that she could bring herself to part with her only child, otherwise a school might have been more advantageous to a girl of such an active and social disposition; but, above all, she pressed Mrs. Hanson to endeavour to preserve in her that spirit of humility which never fails to produce obedience, subdue passion, and open the mind for the reception and nurture of every virtue.

On the arrival of Mrs. Hanson, Mrs. Harewood had left the real improvements of Matilda to be discovered by circumstances; and as the mother and daughter were seldom apart, she had not spoken of the kind and charitable actions which Matilda had performed, fearful of injuring by praise those blossoms which were now only beginning to expand; but she now dilated on them with pleasure, both to the happy mother and Mrs. Weston; and such was the effect of this discourse on the former, that tears of pleasure and gratitude to Heaven ran down her cheek. Matilda, although still engaged with the child, catching a view of her mother under this emotion, could not forbear running up to her, and tenderly inquired what was the matter.

"Nothing at all, my love, at least nothing painful; we have been speaking of you—I am anxious to engage you a governess."

"Well, mamma, and will Mrs. Weston be so good as to undertake me?"

The ladies all started, but by no means with any symptom of dismay, although Mrs. Hanson said, with some confusion, to Mrs. Weston—"My little girl takes a great liberty, ma'am, but you must pardon her premature request; she fancies you are an old friend, I believe, because you are her countrywoman."

"I wish sincerely I had any other claim to being considered her friend, madam, as in that case—"

Mrs. Weston suddenly checked herself, her colour rose, and the tears stood in her eyes.

"Suffer me, my dear friend, to interpret your silence for Mrs. Hanson;—in *that* case you would not object to undertaking

Mrs. Hofland

the charge which Matilda has very innocently, though very abruptly, been willing to assign to you?"

"If you are a faithful interpreter, I will call you a most agreeable one," said Mrs. Hanson, "for Mrs. Weston would be an equal acquisition to both me and my daughter."

Mrs. Weston wiped her eyes—"Believe me, dear ladies," said she, "I am grateful for your good opinion, and truly desirous of profiting by your kind offer; but you are both mothers, and will, I am certain, consider my situation as such. I am but newly arrived; it will take some time to wean my poor child from her habits; and to send one so very young to school, is a painful consideration; in a few months I shall be happy indeed to avail myself of your goodness, and enter with pleasure on so promising a task."

Mrs. Hanson was just going to express her entire approbation of this proposal, when Matilda, with a modest, but earnest air, entreated permission to speak, which was immediately granted.

"Do not think me vain nor presuming, dear Mrs. Weston, if I say, that, whilst you are my governess, I will, with my mamma's permission, become little Harriet's governess; I am quite sure it will do us both a great deal of good, for she will every hour remind me how much more naughty and tiresome and provoking I used to be when I first came over, and teach me to endure with patience, and remove with gentleness and firmness, the errors which, in so young and engaging a child, claim my compassion rather than blame. I shall love her very dearly, I am certain, because I see she is of a loving temper, notwithstanding her faults; and I am certain, if she feels as I do, she will love me for curing her of them; then I will teach her all I know, and as I shall improve every day, you know I shall improve her also! Dear mamma, pray let me try! I do not know any way in which a girl like me can show gratitude to God so effectually, as in endeavouring to make my fellow-creature as happy as myself, and especially my own little countrywoman."

The tenderness and earnestness with which this request was urged, as well as the excellent motive, ensured its success; and in a few days the mother and daughter removed together to Brompton, and a regular system of education was entered upon, which was indeed attended with the most happy effects, although it is probable that Matilda found her new office abound with trials, of which she could form no idea until experience taught her. It is however certain, that she received as much benefit as she communicated, and that she learned the lessons of virtue whilst imparting them to her little pupil, who proved a very tractable and intelligent child, after she had become weaned from those habits which were in a great measure inseparable from her late situation in life. It is probable that but for this stimulus to her exertions, Matilda would have neglected her education, and sunk into indolent habits, for want of those excitements which she had found in the society of Ellen and her brothers; whereas now she endeavoured, at every meeting with this dear family, to exhibit some improvement or attainment in her pupil, and these were inevitably connected with her own.

But notwithstanding the advantages Matilda possessed, and her earnest desire to profit by them, and even the actual improvement she evinced, our young readers must not suppose either that she was perfect, or that she had attained that standard of excellence of which she was capable. Many a moment of petulance occurred with her provoking little pupil, and airs of arrogance were apt to swell her bosom, upon those occasions which called out the superiority of her fortune, or the exhibition of those talents which could not fail to be remarked in her situation of life. But on these occasions it was never difficult for Mrs. Weston or her good mamma to recall her to a sense of the folly and guilt of indulging such a temper; for her religious principles were deeply ingrafted, and her sensibility genuine and active; so that the moment her mind perceived that she was wounding a fellow-creature, and thereby offending God, her heart revolted from her own conduct, and she lost not a moment in retracting the assertions of anger, and rendering, as far as she was able, every atonement for her error.

CHAPTER XIV

Time passed, and the children of either house exhibited those gradual changes which are scarcely perceptible to a parent's eye, under which they so constantly remain. The young men exchanged school for college; the girls, under the protecting guardianship of their mothers, were taken into public; and a new sense of care, on a new ground, pervaded those anxious hearts, which beat but for their beloved offspring, and which were perhaps most solicitous for them, at the time they were indulging the innocent and artless gaiety natural to their age.

As Edmund Harewood had ever been a thoughtful youth, and possessed talents which were likely to render his study of the law beneficial both to himself and the community, Mr. Harewood changed his opinion as to the profession he intended him to pursue, and directed him to prepare for the bar, to the entire satisfaction of the young man.

Charles had for some time evinced a great desire to enter the army; but as his mother could not conquer her feelings, so far as to permit it, he was at length induced to resign the scheme entirely; but his anxiety to travel continuing as strong as ever, Mr. Harewood promised, if possible, to procure him some situation in life which would allow him to indulge his wishes, consistent with his duty; but this was conceded on the express terms of his diligent application to study; and as he perceived himself the positive necessity of becoming a good linguist, he applied himself to learning the modern languages with great assiduity.

Ellen grew up a pretty girl, but her figure was diminutive, and the gentleness and docility which had been ever her happiest characteristic, diffused a charm of feminine softness over her whole person, which was to many very attractive, though not striking. The equanimity of her temper had the effect of perpetuating that smooth and dimpled description of countenance which is peculiar to childhood; so that, although a year older than Matilda, she appeared younger; and when they were seen together among strangers, she was considered as a younger sister, supported by the kind attentions of her superior; for Matilda, although very modest, was dignified, and her person, being elegant and tall, confirmed the idea.

In a short time, Mrs. Hanson received several offers from men of fortune for Matilda, all of which were politely but positively refused; for the poor girl always showed a decided dread of leaving her mother, and very justly observed, that a very intimate acquaintance was necessary between persons who bound themselves to so sacred and indissoluble a connection as marriage; and although naturally too generous and ingenuous to suspect others of acting from unworthy motives, she was yet aware that a young woman who has a large fortune in her own disposal, and who has neither father nor brother to investigate the private character of those who address her, has need of a more than ordinary share of prudence, and will be wise in delaying a consent which deprives her of all control over the wealth of which Providence has appointed her steward.

Although thus wise in her decision on this important point, and ever assigning reasons which showed how utterly unbiassed her affections were towards the candidates for her favour, yet Matilda did not always act with equal wisdom; she was excessively fond of dancing, and as she acquitted herself with uncommon grace, perhaps vanity furnished her with an additional motive for her desire to partake this amusement more frequently than it suited her mamma; and once she accepted an invitation to a private ball, when Mrs. Weston was her chaperon. Waltzing was introduced, and Matilda, though by no means pleased with the general style of the dance, was struck with certain movements which she thought graceful, and the day following began to practise them with her young *protegee*.

"I think you waltz very well," said Mrs. Weston.

"I soon should do so, I dare say, if I practised it; but as it was new to me, I durst not venture last night, although I made a kind of half promise to Sir Theodore Branson, that I would do it the very next time we met."

"Do you call that waltzing?" said Mrs. Hanson, laying down her netting; "it appears to me to be more the work of the hands than the feet a great deal; and you go round and round, child, very foolishly, till one grows giddy to look at you—so, so—well, and what, do the gentlemen stand by to grow giddy too?"

"Dear mamma, the gentlemen waltz with the ladies; I said, you know, that Sir Theodore wished me to do it, but I refused."

"You did perfectly right; I should have been much hurt if you had waltzed with any man."

"It is very fashionable, mother."

"More the pity; but I am sure I need no argument against it to

Mrs. Hofland

you, Matilda."

"Indeed, mamma, I see nothing against it—I think it very graceful; and I am sure, if you had seen Lady Emma Lovell last night, you would have thought so too."

"My admiration of her person would not for a moment have changed my opinion of her conduct. I see beautiful women, who expose their persons in a manner I decidedly condemn (as I know, Matilda, you do likewise); looking at them as fine *statues*, I may admire the work of the great Artificer; but the moment I consider them as *women* filling a respectable place in society, the wives and daughters of men of rank and probity, and, what is still stronger, women professing, at least nominally, to be members of the Christian church, I turn from them with disgust and sorrow; and though I sincerely despise all affectation of more exalted purity than others, I yet will never hesitate to give my voice against a folly so unworthy of my sex, and which can be only tolerated by women whose vanity has destroyed that delicacy which is our best recommendation."

Matilda applied all her mother said to waltzing, and thought it was equally just with the strictures she herself felt true, with regard to the mode of dress adopted by some whom she met in public. Ellen and herself were ever well, and even fashionably, dressed; but yet they avoided the fault they condemned: for some time, the sisterly affection which really subsisted between them, induced them to appear in similar dresses; but as Matilda rose to womanhood, a fear lest Ellen should be induced to expense, added to some jokes that were passed upon her respecting Charles, induced her to forego this plan, and Ellen had too much good sense to pursue it further; and, as the acquaintance of Mrs. Hanson increased, Matilda was necessarily led into parties where Ellen could not meet her; so that they became in some degree divided in person, but their attachment remained the same. Mrs. Hanson was desirous that her daughter should take a more extensive view of society than was necessary for Ellen; she dreaded an early marriage for her, although she thought it desirable to bring her into society, being persuaded that young women of large fortune too frequently are rendered unhappy in the marriage state, by being dazzled at their first outset in life by the novelty, and gaiety of the scene around them, which leads them to expect a continuance of the same brilliant career, incompatible with the duties of that state into which they incautiously plunge; whereas a short time passed in life, would show them the inefficacy of trifling amusement and splendid show to procure real satisfaction, and lead them to investigate those circumstances in the minds and situations of their admirers, most likely to ensure their future felicity, and most consonant with their real wants and wishes. The judicious mother saw, with the truest pleasure, that the well-turned mind of her daughter ever pointed to the scenes of simple enjoyment and virtuous intelligence which illumined her early years; but, in her peculiar situation, she was aware that Matilda, to a certain degree, should adopt the apostle's advice—"Try all things, cleave to that which is good."

On the other hand, Mr. and Mrs. Harewood, as the young people advanced towards maturity, had felt it a point of delicacy, however sincere and ardent their friendship might be, in a slight degree to abstain from that intimate and daily intercourse which had so long and happily subsisted between the families. The days were past when Charles could romp with, or Edmund instruct, Matilda; and although they held the same rank in society, yet as the noble fortune of Matilda (increased materially by the retired way in which her mother lived during her infancy) entitled her to marry a nobleman, Mr. Harewood did not choose that the presence of his sons should cause reports which might prevent her from receiving offers of this nature. He was attached to Matilda, as if she had indeed been his child, but he was too independent, as well as too honest, to render either his present affection, or his past services, the medium of increasing the general regard Matilda had manifested for both his sons into a decided predilection for either: nor was he aware that either of the young men had for her that peculiar attachment which a man ought to feel for a wife. Edmund was wrapt *apparently* in a profession which is in its own nature absorbing, and Charles appeared too eager to travel to have any tendency to early marriage.

About a week after the foregoing conversation had taken place between Matilda and her mother, the former went again to a ball, with a lady of rank, who engaged to be her guardian for the night, as Mrs. Hanson and Mrs. Weston had both caught severe colds, from being out late together.

Lady Araminta Montague, the conductor of Matilda for the evening, was a fashionable and showy woman, who never appeared in public without being surrounded by all those who affected to be considered persons of taste, and fitted to move in the first style. She was now sought with more than common avidity, on account of her attractive companion, whom she endeavoured to show off in the happiest manner, by leading the light conversation of the moment to subjects familiar to Matilda's observation, or likely to draw from her those remarks in which the ability and talent she possessed would be naturally, yet strikingly, displayed. Of this species of kindness Matilda was wholly unconscious, as it was one which her own friends had never adopted; when, therefore, she found herself the universal centre of attraction in the room, it was no wonder that her spirits were unusually elated, and her vanity took the lead; so that when the sprightly dance added its intoxicating powers, and her mind was entranced by the pleasure of the moment, she forgot the resolutions and opinions formed in a wiser hour.

When the first two country-dances were over, several parties began, as on the preceding night, to form into couples for the purpose of waltzing, at that time a novelty in this country; and while Matilda was looking at them, to her surprise, Sir Theodore Branson just entered the room, and asked the honour of her hand, which he almost claimed as a promise.

This young gentleman was considered the handsomest man, and the most elegant dancer, in the circles of fashion. That he was at once a shallow coxcomb and an encroaching acquaintance, unfortunately did not prevent many young ladies from desiring him as a partner; and when Matilda perceived the leer of envy, and the pause of observation directed towards her, she half gave him her hand, being conscious that her own figure and style of dancing would be superior to any other of the candidates for admiration that had preceded her; yet she paused, remembering her mother's words, and, with a kind of anxious, fearful gaze, that fell like a veil over the exultation and gaiety of her features, she looked an appeal to the lady who was her guide, or ought to have been.

"Really, my dear, I don't know what to say; but as the thing is new, if you are not quite *au fait*, you will be pardoned, and Sir Theodore is so admirable a partner, I really think you may venture to try."

Matilda, in a calmer moment, would have seen how totally distinct her ladyship's fears were from those of her mother; but the flutter of her spirits, the demands of her vanity, and the address of her partner, combined to hurry her forward, and she found herself in the midst of the group before she was aware: it was then too late to recede: the motion for a short time restored her spirits; but as the arm of Sir Theodore encircled her waist, deep confusion overwhelmed her, she blushed to a degree that was absolutely painful; and though unable, in the hurry of the motion, to entertain a positive reflection, yet a thousand thoughts seemed to press at once for admittance, all tinged with self-reproach; and at length, unable to endure them, she suddenly laid her hand upon her forehead, and ran, or rather reeled, to her seat.

As it was the nature of the dance to produce the sensation of dizziness, this circumstance excited no particular attention, and her partner merely rallied her upon it, with that air of *badinage* young men now-a-days pretty generally adopt. Every word he uttered was distressing to Matilda, who felt as if she were insulted by his freedom, and had degraded herself too far to enjoy the right of resenting it; her native pride, however, contending with her self-condemnation, she removed her hand from her eyes, in order to give him a look which would repel his impertinence, and, to her utter astonishment, saw three gentlemen standing before, and looking earnestly upon her; two of these were her friends, Edmund and Charles Harewood.

The moment she looked up, the first withdrew, but Charles and the stranger advanced; they did not, however, find it very easy to approach her, guarded as she was by the officious Sir Theodore; but as Charles was not easily balked in any intention he had formed, he succeeded in inquiring after her health, and introducing his friend Mr. Belmont to her.

"I am very glad—I mean I did not know you were here," said Matilda confusedly.

"Mr. Belmont introduced us. We only arrived from Oxford yesterday, and Ellen, being very anxious that Mr. Belmont should see you, proposed our coming hither."

A little relieved from observing that Edmund still did not join them, under whose eye she felt that she should have shrunk, Matilda ventured to look at Mr. Belmont, recollecting that she had frequently heard him mentioned as the friend of both the brothers, during their residence at Oxford, and that he had been the visitant of the family the preceding winter, when she was on an excursion to Bath; she knew that he was highly esteemed by the family, and, aware in what a favourable point of view their affection for her would lead them to represent her, the idea that her first introduction had taken place at a moment which, of all others, she most regretted, was really insupportable to her.

Lady Araminta endeavoured, by her praise, to remove the chagrin which her ingenuous countenance (ever the faithful harbinger of her thoughts) betrayed so plainly—"I assure you, my dear," said she, "that for some time you performed very prettily; didn't you think so, Mr. Harewood?"

"Pardon me, my lady, from differing with you—I have seen a country actress do it much better: indeed I said so at the moment—Belmont knows I did; and my brother observed that—"

At this moment the country-dance was recommenced, and Matilda was hurried away, although her solicitude to hear what Edmund said amounted to misery; but as Charles was addressing Lady Araminta, not her, it was impossible to ask; besides, no small portion of anger at Edmund mingled with her anxiety—he had never yet approached her. She knew indeed that his ideas of feminine decorum were rigid; but still he had no right to resent her conduct, or he might have told her as a friend, as he used to do, wherein she erred. As these thoughts struck upon her mind, he passed her in the dance, and made her a profound bow of recognition; she watched to the bottom, and perceived him engaged in earnest conversation with a very lovely young person, whom she remembered as one of those who refused to waltz; again her heart smote her, yet her anger was the most predominant emotion, and she felt as if Edmund Harewood had injured her beyond forgiveness.

The waltzing recommenced, but the very name of it was now hateful to Matilda, and she hastily entreated Lady Araminta to order her carriage. Charles was near; accustomed to read her thoughts, he advanced to offer his hand to lead her down stairs—"You are not well, Matilda," said he, tenderly—"at least not comfortable—I am sure you are not."

Matilda replied only by a smothered sigh.

"They tell me," continued Charles, "that you are about to marry Sir Theodore Branson?"

"'Tis false," said Matilda, quickly, her bosom evidently palpitating with shame and anger.

"Then how could you think of waltzing with him? I am sure neither Edmund nor myself would have dared (brothers as we once deemed ourselves) to have taken—but—really I beg pardon, Miss Hanson; while I condemn another, I intrude too far myself."

Matilda was just stepping into the carriage; she turned her eyes on Charles—they were full of tears, tears such as he had seen in her repentant eyes in early days; he was affected with them—he felt that the latter part of his speech had hurt her—that she was not the fashionable belle, but still the good girl he must love and admire.—"Then," cried he, eagerly, "you will not marry that sprig of a baronet—eh, Matilda?"

"I will not *indeed*."

"And do you not mean to waltz again?"

"No; I was a fool once, but—"

The carriage drove off, and Charles returned with a light heart to the ball-room; but that of Edmund was very heavy, and the friends shortly left the gay scene, and returned to Mr. Harewood's.

CHAPTER XV

"I will never go any where again without you, indeed, mother, I am determined," said Matilda, with a sorrowful air, the following morning.

This was the prelude to a confession of error, which in part relieved the mind of Matilda: but she was still uneasy—she felt as if Charles would be her apologist with his family, for an error they were likely to blame in her; but the ardour of his manner made her feel much concerned for *him*—he was dear to her—she felt for him a sister's affection, but felt that she could never be more to him than she was then. Anxious and restless, she earnestly desired to see Ellen, whose gentleness and dispassionate good sense would soothe the fretfulness and allay the uneasiness she felt; yet she could not bring herself to call on the family—she had not the courage to meet Mr. and Mrs. Harewood, nor the calmness with which she desired to see the brothers. While she was debating what course to pursue, to her infinite relief she heard that Ellen had just called with her father, and that both of them were in the library. Before she had time to welcome them, Ellen, running up stairs, hurried with her into the dressing-room, and closed the door with an air of secrecy which showed her expectation of giving or receiving intelligence of importance, and there was in her countenance an expression which combined both joy and sorrow, and was really indefinable.

Full of her own cares, and anxious to conceal the most interesting part of them, Matilda for some time remained silent, nor did Ellen find the courage requisite for her own communication; so that this much desired visit promised little eventual satisfaction. To account for the situation of Ellen, it is necessary to trace the events of the morning in her father's house.

When the family were assembled to breakfast, the conversation naturally turned upon the ball of the evening before; and Ellen, with friendly zeal, sought to exculpate her friend Matilda from the errors which Mr. Belmont seemed to think her guilty of, in exhibiting herself in a dance, by no means decorous, with a young man of Sir Theodore's description.— "I do not say," added he, "that it was a positively wrong thing, nor do I much wonder at it; for a fine young woman, and an heiress, may be led a great way, by the flatterers and sycophants who surround her; but I must own I expected better things from the chosen friend of Ellen Harewood, from a girl educated by a pious and sensible mother, and one said to possess a sound understanding."

Edmund was silent, but his varying complexion bespoke the strong interest he felt in the subject; Charles, on the contrary, warmly entered into it, declaring that a few words which passed between Matilda and him clearly proved that she had been misled by her party; that her sense of propriety was as strong as ever; and, in short, that she was a dear, amiable, good girl, whom he would defend as long as he lived.

The warmth of Charles's assertion called a smile from every one. During the time he spoke, his father had been called out; the servant now entered, desiring *his* presence also; and it appeared that their early visitant was a man of great importance, and the cause of his calling at this time, by awakening curiosity, suspended conversation. In a few minutes he departed, and Mr. Harewood returned to the breakfast-room, saying as he entered—"I am going to announce a piece of excellent news, although it is accompanied by a loss we must submit to; our dear Charles is appointed to be secretary to the embassy to—, now preparing to embark."

Mrs. Harewood burst into tears; but as soon as she could speak, she expressed her joy, while Ellen, in a broken voice, exclaimed—"Oh, what will Matilda say, poor girl?"

Edmund rushed out of the room, as if to seek his brother, but Mr. Belmont well knew it was to conceal his emotion; no other person seemed to notice Ellen's unfortunate ejaculation, and when the door was closed, Mr. Belmont congratulated the parents upon a circumstance so honourable and desirable to their younger son; and as they well knew the sincerity of his character, and the affection he felt for Charles, they freely confided to him their feelings at the event; while Ellen innocently declared that she was very glad he happened to be with them at the time, as he would be a substitute for dear Charles.

"Ah!" said Mr. Belmont, "if you, Ellen, could persuade your parents, and, what is in this case of more importance, your *own* heart, to consider me not only now, but ever, a member of your family, I should be happy indeed."

Ellen, rather surprised at this speech than its import, for she had long half hoped, half feared, to think on this interesting but awful subject, turned to her mother, and hid her blushing cheek upon her shoulder, while the parents exchanged looks of satisfaction with each other, and esteem towards the speaker.

"Mine, Ellen," continued Mr. Belmont, "is neither a sudden nor violent passion; I approach you by no flattery—I dazzle you by no exhibition; but as I trust both my fortune and character will bear the scrutiny of your friends, your only task, my sweet girl, is to examine your own heart, and inquire there how far I am agreeable to your wishes. I have been a silent admirer of your virtues, and I can be a patient attendant for your decision."

Ellen gave one glance towards her mother—it answered all her wishes; she turned, deeply blushing, to Mr. Belmont, and timidly, yet with an air of perfect confidence, tendered him her hand; she would have spoken, but the variety of emotion so suddenly called forth by the departure of her brother, and the declaration of her lover, overpowered her, and he received thus a silent, but a full consent to his wishes.

In the mean time, Edmund had conquered the more immediate pang that laboured at his heart, and, entering the library, had grasped the hand of Charles, and uttered a few words of congratulation, but it was in a voice so broken, that there was more of sorrow than joy in it.

Charles had not the slightest doubt of his brother's affection, he did not therefore doubt for a moment the sincerity of his assertion, but he was persuaded that the idea of his own situation, as being two years older, and yet likely to remain dependent on his father for some years, was a sensible mortification to him; and, feeling for his situation, he said— "Ay, my dear fellow, there is a difference between us *now*, sure enough; but there is no doubt of your doing well by and by; besides, you are the eldest, and deserve to be so; I am sure father can never do too much for such a son as you are, Edmund."

Edmund gazed in astonishment to hear Charles express

himself with so much ease, at a time when he expected his heart must be overpowered with trouble; his fears lately excited by the agitation and warmth with which Charles had vindicated Matilda, and the unguarded exclamation of Ellen, who evidently thought her younger brother the favourite, now took another turn; he surveyed Charles; he was just twenty-three—a tall, handsome young man, and one who had ever been admired by the ladies. "Perhaps," said he, "internally, poor Matilda loves him, but without having her affection returned: this accounts for the many great offers she has refused, for the sympathy of Ellen, who knows her heart, and for the vindication she undoubtedly made to him last night; whereas to *me* she was cold and unintelligible."

While these painful thoughts rankled in the mind of the young barrister, his happy brother was flying all over the house, receiving from the servants the mixed congratulation of joy in his success and sorrow for his departure; he had also joined the *coterie* in the parlour, wrung the hand of his future brother-in-law, kissed his mother and Ellen, and thanked his father twenty times for all his generous cares, before Edmund could muster philosophy enough to join the family, and listen to its arrangements for the day.

It was at length agreed that Edmund should assist his mother in making up a package of books, &c., for the traveller, who, accompanied by Belmont, should visit the city for necessary arrangements; and Mr. Harewood, who knew that Ellen would naturally wish to see Matilda, agreed to accompany her thither, being at once desirous to communicate this various intelligence to Mrs. Hanson, and to witness the effect Charles's departure would have upon Matilda, whom, at the bottom of his heart, he certainly desired to have for a daughter, although he would have rejoiced in her alliance with any worthy man.

We return now to the young ladies in the dressing-room, each eager to hear and to speak, yet each oppressed, though very differently, with solicitude. At length, Ellen, her breast labouring with sighs, and fear lest she should wound the heart of her friend, thus spoke: "We are going to lose Charles: he has got an appointment, Matilda."

"And is he pleased with it, Ellen?"

"Oh, yes! he seems quite happy: he is running all over the house, just in his old way, and the servants are all laughing and crying about him, as if he were still a school-boy."

"I am heartily glad of it—he has my sincerest good wishes, and I feel certain of his success."

Ellen looked in the face of Matilda, to see if she did *indeed* rejoice; she perceived a tear twinkle in the corner of her young friend's eye, but it was not the tear of sorrow. Ellen could now read the heart on subjects of this kind; she felt that she had been completely mistaken in Matilda's supposed predilection, and she was almost sorry to see her so happy.

"There is a—a—another affair going on at our house," said Ellen, after a pause.

Matilda felt her heart beat with unusual violence; she could not speak, but her very soul peeped out of her eyes to say— "What is it?"

"It is not a parting; it—it—is a joining."

"Oh," said Matilda, calling all her fortitude to her aid, "you are going to have a wedding, eh?"

"I believe it will come to that, indeed, some time."

Matilda turned as pale as death; but her colour rushed suddenly back to her cheeks, as at this moment the door opened, and Mr. Harewood and Mrs. Hanson broke on their *tete-a-tete*. The former felt assured that poor Matilda had heard the destination of Charles, and was suffering under it; but as he could hardly believe Mrs. Hanson would consent to her marriage with his youngest son, and as he thought Charles himself had no thoughts of marriage at this time, he could not allow himself to rejoice in her predilection. To relieve her, he said—"Well, my dear, you heard how we are situated, some of us parting for a time, some uniting for ever; I am sure you rejoice in all that is good, in either of these cases."

Matilda, overpowered, burst into sudden tears.

"My daughter is very nervous this morning," said Mrs. Hanson; "she cannot help being affected with such material changes in the state of those she loves so well; you are aware her tears are those of joy, Mr. Harewood."

Matilda struggled to recover her composure, and, turning to Mr. Harewood, she put both her hands into his, and said, with a low but earnest voice—"My dear, *dear* sir, I do most truly rejoice in the prospect of any good that can befall your family; I saw the—the young lady—the bride-elect—she is very pretty—I hope she will be as good as she is handsome; and I—"

Matilda suddenly stopped, unable to articulate the rest of her good wishes, and Mr. Harewood eagerly said—"As to *that* we will say nothing; I trust Ellen will make a good wife; I am sure she has had a good example."

"*Ellen!*" screamed Matilda; "is it you, Ellen? *you* that are going to be married—you?"

"Dear me, how astonished you look! I suppose I shall be married some time. I told you that perhaps Mr. Belmont might, *some time*—"

"My dear, *dear* Ellen, pardon my dulness, and accept my sincerest congratulations. May Heaven bless you, and him you prefer, and make you both as happy as you deserve to be!"

"So, so!" cried Mr. Harewood; "if we had never come up stairs, this mighty secret, which, for my part, I told an hour ago down stairs, would never have been revealed. But pray, Matilda, who did you conclude was the marrying person at our house, if it were not Ellen?"

"You have sons, sir," tremulously articulated Matilda, not choosing to trust her tongue with a name that dwelt ever on her heart.

"Oh, tut, tut, there is no marrying for my boys. Charles is disposed of, and if Edmund can take a wife at thirty, he will be better off than many in his profession; he is now but a little past five-and-twenty, you know."

"He danced with a very beautiful woman last night," said Matilda, eagerly, and with recovered vivacity.

"So I understand; she is a bride, and his first fee was given for a consultation on her marriage-settlements."

Matilda breathed; the lustre of her eye, the glow on her cheek, could not be mistaken by the fond parent, who now clearly understood the cause of Matilda's frequent despondency, and the refusals she had given to all offers of marriage.

"I wish," said Mrs. Hanson, "that you and Mrs. Harewood

Mrs. Hofland

and our young friends would dine with me: I am really impatient to be introduced to Mr. Belmont."

"As you please, madam; the wanderer must certainly see you once more, and I do not know that he can choose a better day."

Ellen proposed writing a note to her mother, and left the room with Mrs. Hanson, when Mr. Harewood, perceiving that Matilda was again in confusion, said, by way of diverting her attention—"You have seen Mr. Belmont, Miss Hanson?"

"Yes, I have; and *he* has seen *me*, to my sorrow. You remind me of a folly I have by no means forgiven in myself. I still want the eye of a tutor, you see."

"Charles has, however, been your advocate so effectually, that I believe not one of the family will ever remember it again."

"Not *one!*" said Matilda, blushing deeply.

"Not *one!* Charles is a warm advocate."

"He is a dear good boy, and always was; I love him very much, and while I rejoice in his good fortune, I shall be sorry to part with him."

Matilda's frankness assured Mr. Harewood that her heart was free where he had supposed it bound; he was anxious to read her farther; he saw that she even sought investigation from him, in whom she confided as a friend and father; but he again shrunk from the idea of undue influence, and while he walked about irresolute, time passed, and Edmund and his mother entered the drawing-room, and Matilda was called to receive them.

An air of coldness and restraint pervaded the manners of both Edmund and Matilda, to divert which, Mrs. Hanson began to relate the error into which her daughter had fallen, from the *mauvaise honte* of Ellen, as she supposed, and this led them to speak of the ball, and the characters of the persons present. Of course, poor Matilda was again tormented by hearing that Sir Theodore was universally believed to be her affianced lover, and she expressed the most unqualified vexation at the report, declaring that she would not go once into public again for seven years, rather than encourage the presumption of the man, or the idle gossip of his admirers.

As she spoke, Edmund was observed to gaze upon her with delight, and exult in the declaration, as if it were necessary for his happiness; but when she ceased to speak, he relapsed into melancholy.

"The only way to silence such reports effectually," said Mrs. Hanson, with a tender smile, "will be to place yourself under the protection of some worthy man, whose character you can indeed approve. I have ever objected to your marrying under age, but I have no objection at all to your gaining liberty, and relinquishing it at the same time. I hope, therefore, in another year, to see you follow the example of Ellen, provided you can choose as well as she has done."

"It is the only thing in which I cannot obey you, my dear mother," replied Matilda.

Hurt with the extreme paleness which overspread the countenance of their inestimable son, Mr. and Mrs. Harewood withdrew to the window; and Ellen, whose heart wanted a pretext for watching the arrival of Belmont, joined

Mrs. Hofland

them; when Mrs. Hanson, drawing closer to Edmund, said—"I fear you will not soon join these marrying people, my young friend?"

"I shall never marry, madam," answered he abruptly.

"*Never!* you are too positive, sir; men at your age change their minds frequently."

"Matilda knows that I am not subject to change; she may accuse me of many errors, but not of that."

"I can accuse *you* of *nothing*," said Matilda; "I wish you could say the same of me."

"Matilda! Miss Hanson! I accuse you! what right have I to accuse you?"

"Every right. I behaved ill—you condemned me—I saw you did; and—you punished me. I felt your punishment last night—to-day you forgive me; and your forgiveness is—why should I not own it? is dear to me."

"Oh, Matilda, do not distract me by this generosity! you will throw me off my guard—you will induce me to make a declaration that may part us for ever."

Edmund looked at Mrs. Hanson; her brow was open, pleasure swam in her eye, and she held her hand towards him as she said—"My dear Edmund, allow me to ask what you mean by that look of mistrust to me? what right have you to suppose that I am less generous than yourself, or that I desire to see my child ungrateful to her young preceptor, or insensible of his merits?"

"Madam! Matilda! what does all this mean? is it possible that

I can have obtained such an advocate as Mrs. Hanson?"

"Edmund, can you really want an advocate with poor erring Matilda? or can you for a moment accuse her of a fault, which never yet came amongst the numerous catalogue of her early sins?"

Mrs. Hanson joined the group at the window, and in a few moments they all descended together, to welcome Charles and Belmont, who soon understood the happy footing on which those so dear to them were placed; and Charles enjoyed a hearty laugh at the jealousy he had excited, though he could not regret a circumstance which had in any measure led to a conclusion so desirable.

When poor Zebby, whose sable forehead was now shaded by gray locks, was told all that had happened, she exclaimed with her usual enthusiasm,—"All right—all happy—Missy have goodee friend, goodee husban—him alway mild and kind; Missy very goodee too—some time little warm, but never, *never* when she lookee at massa; him melt her heart, guide her steps, both go hand in hand to heaven."

The negro's conception of this union has every prospect of being verified, and proves that the simplest and most uninformed of human beings may yet enjoy the light of reason, and a just perception of the characters of those around them.

When Charles had bade adieu to his family, the lovers of Matilda and Ellen were each urgent for their respective marriages: but the awfulness of that sacred engagement into which they were about to enter, the consciousness they entertained of the goodness of their parents, and the happiness of the state they were quitting, held the young ladies for some time in a state of apparent suspense, and almost incertitude.

This was neither the effect of want of confidence in the men they loved, nor of that spirit of coquetry by which the vain and frivolous part of the sex seek to prolong what they consider the day of their power. Far different ideas pervaded their minds and influenced their conduct; for not only the tenderness of their affection for their parents, but the sense of their responsibility as Christian wives, called to new duties and new avocations, appointed to guide their inferiors, and submit to their future husbands, pressed upon their hearts; and when at length the solemn ceremony took place, it was to each party rather a day of serious thoughtfulness and fearful anxiety, than one of exultation and exhibition.

In a short time this solicitude vanished, and a sense of happiness, confidence, and unbounded affection spread over their minds the most delightful serenity, and rendered every act of duty an act of pleasure. Matilda looked to Edmund as the guardian of her conduct, and he found in her the reward of his virtues, the companion whose vivacity enlivened the fatigue of study, and whose benevolence extended the circle of his enjoyments; and although apparently of very different tempers, the affection they felt for each other, and the well-regulated minds they both possessed, rendered them proverbially good and happy.

After residing a few years abroad, and increasing his knowledge and reputation, Charles returned, and is now become the husband of Miss Weston, who is an amiable and virtuous young woman, well calculated to render him happy. The mother of this young lady still resides with Mrs. Hanson, to whom her society is particularly valuable, since the removal of Matilda, whose eldest child is the frequent inmate of her house.

Happy in themselves, and a blessing to the circle around them, Mr. and Mrs. Belmont reside during the greatest part of the year upon the family estate of Mr. Belmont in Staffordshire. Ellen, as a country gentlewoman, extends a quiet but beneficial influence through an extensive neighbourhood, and is universally beloved and respected.

We will now take leave of the Barbadoes Girl and her friends, with the sincere wish that all who read her story may, like her, endeavour to correct in themselves those irregularities of temper, and proneness to pride and vanity, which, more or less, are the growth of every human heart, and which can never rise and flourish there, but to the destruction of every virtue and every comfort; and we earnestly desire them to hold in mind, that, in order to purify the heart from these unhallowed guests, a deep sense of religion must be the motive, and a strict principle of self-control the agent, by which so desirable an end can alone be obtained.

This little story, written rather to instruct than amuse, can only close with consistency, by briefly recapitulating the lesson it has, perhaps feebly, but sincerely, endeavoured to inculcate, viz., the necessity of watchfulness over our hearts —the excellence and advantage of being open and ingenuous —the efficacy of repentance towards God, and humility even towards man—and the peculiar necessity of guarding the heart, as with a tenfold barrier, to those who are blest with riches and prosperity.

Mrs. Hofland

Choose from Thousands of 1stWorldLibrary Classics By

A. M. Barnard
Ada Leverson
Adolphus William Ward
Aesop
Agatha Christie
Alexander Aaronsohn
Alexander Kielland
Alexandre Dumas
Alfred Gatty
Alfred Ollivant
Alice Duer Miller
Alice Turner Curtis
Alice Dunbar
Allen Chapman
Alleyne Ireland
Ambrose Bierce
Amelia E. Barr
Amory H. Bradford
Andrew Lang
Andrew McFarland Davis
Andy Adams
Angela Brazil
Anna Alice Chapin
Anna Sewell
Annie Besant
Annie Hamilton Donnell
Annie Payson Call
Annie Roe Carr
Annonaymous
Anton Chekhov
Archibald Lee Fletcher
Arnold Bennett
Arthur C. Benson
Arthur Conan Doyle
Arthur M. Winfield
Arthur Ransome
Arthur Schnitzler
Arthur Train
Atticus
B.H. Baden-Powell
B. M. Bower
B. C. Chatterjee
Baroness Emmuska Orczy
Baroness Orczy
Basil King
Bayard Taylor
Ben Macomber
Bertha Muzzy Bower
Bjornstjerne Bjornson

Booth Tarkington
Boyd Cable
Bram Stoker
C. Collodi
C. E. Orr
C. M. Ingleby
Carolyn Wells
Catherine Parr Traill
Charles A. Eastman
Charles Amory Beach
Charles Dickens
Charles Dudley Warner
Charles Farrar Browne
Charles Ives
Charles Kingsley
Charles Klein
Charles Hanson Towne
Charles Lathrop Pack
Charles Romyn Dake
Charles Whibley
Charles Willing Beale
Charlotte M. Braeme
Charlotte M. Yonge
Charlotte Perkins Stetson
Clair W. Hayes
Clarence Day Jr.
Clarence E. Mulford
Clemence Housman
Confucius
Coningsby Dawson
Cornelis DeWitt Wilcox
Cyril Burleigh
D. H. Lawrence
Daniel Defoe
David Garnett
Dinah Craik
Don Carlos Janes
Donald Keyhoe
Dorothy Kilner
Dougan Clark
Douglas Fairbanks
E. Nesbit
E. P. Roe
E. Phillips Oppenheim
E. S. Brooks
Earl Barnes
Edgar Rice Burroughs
Edith Van Dyne
Edith Wharton

Edward Everett Hale
Edward J. O'Biren
Edward S. Ellis
Edwin L. Arnold
Eleanor Atkins
Eleanor Hallowell Abbott
Eliot Gregory
Elizabeth Gaskell
Elizabeth McCracken
Elizabeth Von Arnim
Ellem Key
Emerson Hough
Emilie F. Carlen
Emily Bronte
Emily Dickinson
Enid Bagnold
Enilor Macartney Lane
Erasmus W. Jones
Ernie Howard Pie
Ethel May Dell
Ethel Turner
Ethel Watts Mumford
Eugene Sue
Eugenie Foa
Eugene Wood
Eustace Hale Ball
Evelyn Everett-green
Everard Cotes
F. H. Cheley
F. J. Cross
F. Marion Crawford
Fannie E. Newberry
Federick Austin Ogg
Ferdinand Ossendowski
Fergus Hume
Florence A. Kilpatrick
Fremont B. Deering
Francis Bacon
Francis Darwin
Frances Hodgson Burnett
Frances Parkinson Keyes
Frank Gee Patchin
Frank Harris
Frank Jewett Mather
Frank L. Packard
Frank V. Webster
Frederic Stewart Isham
Frederick Trevor Hill
Frederick Winslow Taylor

Friedrich Kerst
Friedrich Nietzsche
Fyodor Dostoyevsky
G.A. Henty
G.K. Chesterton
Gabrielle E. Jackson
Garrett P. Serviss
Gaston Leroux
George A. Warren
George Ade
Geroge Bernard Shaw
George Cary Eggleston
George Durston
George Ebers
George Eliot
George Gissing
George MacDonald
George Meredith
George Orwell
George Sylvester Viereck
George Tucker
George W. Cable
George Wharton James
Gertrude Atherton
Gordon Casserly
Grace E. King
Grace Gallatin
Grace Greenwood
Grant Allen
Guillermo A. Sherwell
Gulielma Zollinger
Gustav Flaubert
H. A. Cody
H. B. Irving
H.C. Bailey
H. G. Wells
H. H. Munro
H. Irving Hancock
H. R. Naylor
H. Rider Haggard
H. W. C. Davis
Haldeman Julius
Hall Caine
Hamilton Wright Mabie
Hans Christian Andersen
Harold Avery
Harold McGrath
Harriet Beecher Stowe
Harry Castlemon
Harry Coghill
Harry Houidini

Hayden Carruth
Helent Hunt Jackson
Helen Nicolay
Hendrik Conscience
Hendy David Thoreau
Henri Barbusse
Henrik Ibsen
Henry Adams
Henry Ford
Henry Frost
Henry James
Henry Jones Ford
Henry Seton Merriman
Henry W Longfellow
Herbert A. Giles
Herbert Carter
Herbert N. Casson
Herman Hesse
Hildegard G. Frey
Homer
Honore De Balzac
Horace B. Day
Horace Walpole
Horatio Alger Jr.
Howard Pyle
Howard R. Garis
Hugh Lofting
Hugh Walpole
Humphry Ward
Ian Maclaren
Inez Haynes Gillmore
Irving Bacheller
Isabel Cecilia Williams
Isabel Hornibrook
Israel Abrahams
Ivan Turgenev
J.G.Austin
J. Henri Fabre
J. M. Barrie
J. M. Walsh
J. Macdonald Oxley
J. R. Miller
J. S. Fletcher
J. S. Knowles
J. Storer Clouston
J. W. Duffield
Jack London
Jacob Abbott
James Allen
James Andrews
James Baldwin

James Branch Cabell
James DeMille
James Joyce
James Lane Allen
James Lane Allen
James Oliver Curwood
James Oppenheim
James Otis
James R. Driscoll
Jane Abbott
Jane Austen
Jane L. Stewart
Janet Aldridge
Jens Peter Jacobsen
Jerome K. Jerome
Jessie Graham Flower
John Buchan
John Burroughs
John Cournos
John F. Kennedy
John Gay
John Glasworthy
John Habberton
John Joy Bell
John Kendrick Bangs
John Milton
John Philip Sousa
John Taintor Foote
Jonas Lauritz Idemil Lie
Jonathan Swift
Joseph A. Altsheler
Joseph Carey
Joseph Conrad
Joseph E. Badger Jr
Joseph Hergesheimer
Joseph Jacobs
Jules Vernes
Julian Hawthrone
Julie A Lippmann
Justin Huntly McCarthy
Kakuzo Okakura
Karle Wilson Baker
Kate Chopin
Kenneth Grahame
Kenneth McGaffey
Kate Langley Bosher
Kate Langley Bosher
Katherine Cecil Thurston
Katherine Stokes
L. A. Abbot
L. T. Meade

L. Frank Baum
Latta Griswold
Laura Dent Crane
Laura Lee Hope
Laurence Housman
Lawrence Beasley
Leo Tolstoy
Leonid Andreyev
Lewis Carroll
Lewis Sperry Chafer
Lilian Bell
Lloyd Osbourne
Louis Hughes
Louis Joseph Vance
Louis Tracy
Louisa May Alcott
Lucy Fitch Perkins
Lucy Maud Montgomery
Luther Benson
Lydia Miller Middleton
Lyndon Orr
M. Corvus
M. H. Adams
Margaret E. Sangster
Margret Howth
Margaret Vandercook
Margaret W. Hungerford
Margret Penrose
Maria Edgeworth
Maria Thompson Daviess
Mariano Azuela
Marion Polk Angellotti
Mark Overton
Mark Twain
Mary Austin
Mary Catherine Crowley
Mary Cole
Mary Hastings Bradley
Mary Roberts Rinehart
Mary Rowlandson
M. Wollstonecraft Shelley
Maud Lindsay
Max Beerbohm
Myra Kelly
Nathaniel Hawthrone
Nicolo Machiavelli
O. F. Walton
Oscar Wilde

Owen Johnson
P.G. Wodehouse
Paul and Mabel Thorne
Paul G. Tomlinson
Paul Severing
Percy Brebner
Percy Keese Fitzhugh
Peter B. Kyne
Plato
Quincy Allen
R. Derby Holmes
R. L. Stevenson
R. S. Ball
Rabindranath Tagore
Rahul Alvares
Ralph Bonehill
Ralph Henry Barbour
Ralph Victor
Ralph Waldo Emmerson
Rene Descartes
Ray Cummings
Rex Beach
Rex E. Beach
Richard Harding Davis
Richard Jefferies
Richard Le Gallienne
Robert Barr
Robert Frost
Robert Gordon Anderson
Robert L. Drake
Robert Lansing
Robert Lynd
Robert Michael Ballantyne
Robert W. Chambers
Rosa Nouchette Carey
Rudyard Kipling
Saint Augustine
Samuel B. Allison
Samuel Hopkins Adams
Sarah Bernhardt
Sarah C. Hallowell
Selma Lagerlof
Sherwood Anderson
Sigmund Freud
Standish O'Grady
Stanley Weyman
Stella Benson
Stella M. Francis

Stephen Crane
Stewart Edward White
Stijn Streuvels
Swami Abhedananda
Swami Parmananda
T. S. Ackland
T. S. Arthur
The Princess Der Ling
Thomas A. Janvier
Thomas A Kempis
Thomas Anderton
Thomas Bailey Aldrich
Thomas Bulfinch
Thomas De Quincey
Thomas Dixon
Thomas H. Huxley
Thomas Hardy
Thomas More
Thornton W. Burgess
U. S. Grant
Upton Sinclair
Valentine Williams
Various Authors
Vaughan Kester
Victor Appleton
Victor G. Durham
Victoria Cross
Virginia Woolf
Wadsworth Camp
Walter Camp
Walter Scott
Washington Irving
Wilbur Lawton
Wilkie Collins
Willa Cather
Willard F. Baker
William Dean Howells
William le Queux
W. Makepeace Thackeray
William W. Walter
William Shakespeare
Winston Churchill
Yei Theodora Ozaki
Yogi Ramacharaka
Young E. Allison
Zane Grey